BASICS

BASICS

A Program Designed to Help You Recognize and Enhance Your Child's Abilities

James J. A. Cavanaugh, M.D.

A Birch Lane Press Book
Published by Carol Publishing Group

A Birch Lane Press Book
Published by Carol Publishing Group

Birch Lane Press is a registered trademark of Carol Communications, Inc.

Editorial Offices: 600 Madison Avenue, New York, N.Y. 10022
Sales & Distribution Offices: 120 Enterprise Avenue, Secaucus, N.J. 07094
In Canada: Musson Book Company, a division of General Publishing
    Company, Ltd., Don Mills, Ontario M3B 2T6

Queries regarding rights and permissions should be addressed to Carol
Publishing Group, 600 Madison Avenue, New York, N.Y. 10022

Carol Publishing Group books are available at special discounts for bulk
purchases, for sales promotions, fund raising, or educational purposes.
Special editions can be created to specifications. For details contact:
Special Sales Department, Carol Publishing Group, 120 Enterprise Avenue,
Secaucus, N.J. 07094

Manufactured in the United States of America
10 9 8 7 6 5 4 3 2 1

Library of Congress Cataloging-in-Publication Data

    Basics : a program designed to help you recognize and enhance your
    child's abilities / by James J. A. Cavanaugh.
        p.   cm.
    "A Birch Lane Press book."
    ISBN 1-55972-085-9
    1. Child development.   I. Title.
HQ767.9.C38   1991
649'.1—dc20   91-27424
                                                          CIP

To
CAITRIOINA, BRIANNA, JAMIE, PARKER,
and the legions of children from whom I have
learned and for whom I want a better opportunity

Contents

Acknowledgments

The creation of this book began with the understanding and devotion that my wife, Jeanne, offered me and showered on our five children, insisting that those qualities most desirable in all of us come from constant and patient attention.

There were many in years past who contributed to the interest, dedication, and direction critical to my concern for the child and his fulfillment. Margaret Fitzgibbons Cavanaugh told me that I had the hands of a surgeon, Clara Jobe Cavanaugh showed me the path to respect, and Elizabeth Ward Loughran taught me scholarship.

Throughout my professional life some were more responsible than others in molding and sustaining my lifelong interest in child development, language, and children's learning: Robert Parrott at Georgetown, Lawson Wilkins at the old Harriet Lane at Hopkins, and Leo Burgin at Harvard and Massachusetts General Hospital. Each in his own way helped the evolutionary process that occurred across student, house officer, and fellowship years. Jeanne Chall at the Harvard Graduate School of Education provided me with the opportunity to enter the world of education and reading, and Louise Ames at the Gesell Institute in New Haven supplied insights, and thus another step in the direction that ultimately led to my view of child development and child rearing spelled out across the pages of this book.

There are, of course, many others to whom I owe a debt for the

ACKNOWLEDGMENTS

scholarship they pursued in their work and in their writings that has contributed to our understanding of the developing child.

Hillel Black at Birch Lane Press gave direction to this project, and Bruce Shostak crafted my words into a cohesive product.

Finally, there are my associates, Marshall Stone, Don Scott, and my daughter, MaryJo Cavanaugh Fitzgibbons, who contributed significantly to the BASICS Child Development Project. I am particularly grateful to MaryJo, who has continued to offer her gift in reaching out to children to guide my thoughts and writing in many aspects of this book.

James J. A. Cavanaugh
Osterville, Massachusetts
May 1991

Introduction

Come away, O human child!
To the waters and the wild

. . . .

For the world's more full of weeping than you
*   can understand*
    —from "The Stolen Child,"
    William Butler Yeats

It's a thoroughly enjoyable job to raise a child, but it's hard work, and the work is getting harder. Given the chance, kids love you, hang on your every word, and follow you around in amazement of your knowledge. At least for the first few years of their lives or until things start going wrong. We need to protect against things going wrong, and that takes a plan and a lot of constant work.

For the most part, we all set out with a handful of objectives: to make our children happy, loved, properly educated, and successful. We are often aware of these objectives, but very little thought goes into the development of a workable plan that is likely to realize them. In life very little happens by magic, but many parents depend heavily on magic when it comes to raising their children.

I say this with authority because most of my life has been spent helping parents see that their children grow up learning and developing properly.

Raising a child is all about what the child learns and how he learns it. Some children learn more successfully than others, and, as we are reminded more and more these days, some children have greater opportunity than others to learn.

Fortunately for me, learning was an important part of our household when I was growing up. I have memories, foggy though they may be, of my mother spending hours talking and reading to us children, constantly encouraging us to ask questions. She viewed learning as the most important thing we could do each day.

The real beginnings of this book, which is all about learning, date back to my grandmother. It was her influence that caused me to become a physician. Whenever I was with her, which was quite often, she told me that I had the hands of a surgeon. Grandma was very Irish, so she always had a saying or two to punctuate any point she was making. I was wondering one day how she knew so much about surgeons, when, to the best of my knowledge, she hadn't been sick a day of her very long life. I came to realize that the lesson that she was trying to get across was that there is more than one way to use your hands to earn a living. So I took her advice and became a doctor.

While in medical school, I took a job at a children's home to earn money for my food and lodging. It was there that I developed a strong interest not only in children, but also in the idea of prevention. One of the senior physicians at the home believed that it was just as important to prevent a problem as it was to treat it. Since most of my time and training in pediatric medicine in school and thereafter was focused on the treatment of diseases, that doctor was clearly well ahead of his time in his thinking.

When I eventually went into pediatric practice in a suburb of

Boston, my interests quickly led me to emphasize the idea that a healthy child leads to a healthy adult. I realized that during a child's development he must be given every opportunity to bring his potential to the surface. This means that a child has to be given every opportunity to learn to the best of his ability. Soon the emphasis of my entire practice was on the child's development and how youngsters learn.

Joel was a youngster who was having some problems in school and at home. He was brought to see me, against his will, I might add, by his mother and stepfather. I would describe him as bright, anxious, and a real smart aleck who was at war with parents and teachers alike. At best he was tolerating the visit, but he needed to get the upper hand. He asked me how well I had raised my own kids.

Although Joel's social skills may have been weak, his thinking was pretty good. He explained that his parents, who by any definition were disasters at raising children—and he offered himself and a sister on drugs as examples—had hired me to give them advice on child rearing. He told me that I was, in effect, a professional parent. The best proof of my qualifications for this job was my own family. He reasoned that I'd probably work harder at my own family than with others.

After I told Joel about our five children and what had happened to them, he agreed that I had been successful enough to be worth listening to. I tried to explain to Joel that my wife and I had been fortunate with our children because they failed to hit any serious roadblocks along the way. Furthermore, I told him that there are some basic rules that apply to the job of child rearing. It's not magic.

Ultimately, Joel agreed to do more than listen. He actually went to work and carried out many of my suggestions. He came to terms with his parents and with school, and when last heard of was enjoying college and doing well at it.

The essential ingredients that go into that successful child-rearing effort are time, love, patience, and a lot of common sense. Perhaps all of this can be described as *interaction*. Raising a child takes work. It is helpful if you know what you're doing, and I think it is essential that you know why you're doing it.

This book is about those ingredients and how you as a parent can blend them together into a plan that allows you to lead your child through the growing-up years and turn him or her into a successful adult.

Many doctors have written books on children and child development, or "parenting," as it's called today. To me parenting suggests something fancy, and raising your child should be anything but fancy. It should be plain and simple. Some of those books stress what's wrong with children while others carefully point out the many problems in the life of a child that need fixing. I'm going to assume that your child is okay to begin with and doesn't need fixing. He simply needs some of that time, love, patience and common sense that I mentioned. I'm going to lead you through some steps that will strengthen your own ideas about how you get the potential that is within your youngster to the surface so that you can put his natural ability and creativity to work for him.

At last count there were nearly a thousand books in print on child development. It's my observation, however, that child development hasn't come of age yet. I don't think that we as a nation take it seriously. Physicians, even those who specialize in children, do not stress child rearing as the focus of their care of the growing child. Often they seem to know relatively little about this whole business. Perhaps this is a reflection of our training as physicians, where the emphasis was, and still is, on the care of the sick. Maybe most doctors consider that that's enough without worrying about those children who are healthy.

We in pediatric medicine have found over the past decade that how you raise your child directly influences the overall health and wellness he carries into adult life. The idea of prevention goes well beyond a concern for tomorrow or the next day.

We seem to care very well for our babies and toddlers in today's society, but by the time children are four we expect that someone else is going to do the job for us. It's not so much that we lose interest but that we expect too much of others. In the last twenty-five years we have learned the hard way that teachers and schools don't raise children. Don't expect it of them! You can rely most of the time on your school to develop certain skills in your child, especially those that have to do with the three R's. It is parents and the community that surrounds the child who educate the child.

Think of it this way: children don't have problems, parents do. We should be trying to keep our children from becoming the parents of another generation with worse problems. Often, although we may not intend to do so, we neglect our kids by not doing the right thing at the right time. This kind of invisible child neglect is epidemic in our society. Change must come in the face of hardship, for today we have less time, fewer hands to help, and, in many cases, fewer resources to call upon.

In my own professional life, I brought together an interest in children and in prevention to care for youngsters who had trouble learning and adjusting at school or at home. That involvement got me focused on the child who learns differently. This was twenty-five years ago when few schools were willing to acknowledge such children, let alone do anything about them. I was fortunate to have the opportunity to study learning and child development through some postdoctoral studies at Harvard and Brandeis. Those studies led me to develop several programs in various school systems to recognize and help children who had problems learning, and to develop some special schools for children who needed special services. In all of these cases I recognized early that the quality of the home life, not the quality of the school program, dictated how well the child did at life. That is not to say that smaller classes, individual attention, and some caring from the teacher didn't help the youngster having trouble with school, but the greatest impact on the child's long-term success dealing with life situations came from the home.

This same observation has been made in analyses of the effectiveness of the Head Start programs. In cases where the children involved had strong continuing support from home, the educational achievement they gained from the program was significant. In those instances where the home support for the children was missing, the educational achievement gained from the program was less, and those gains were not sustained. During the past five years in some states, programs have been developed that involve the parents as teachers of their children. These programs have begun to demonstrate success in the educational achievement of the involved children.

As I looked at factors that influence the success of the child in our society I realized that everything points toward regular hands-on interaction between parent and child. The involvement must have direction and cause. It's not enough to love your child. You must guide and instruct your child to develop the capabilities necessary to cope with and succeed at life.

Think of it. No animal in nature abandons its young without insuring that the offspring has a fair shot at survival. We need to do much more than that with our children. I have come full circle in my early interest in children and prevention, from a period of concern with children who had problems with their development to an awareness that parents, particularly the parents of this generation, need to know not how to treat problems, but how to prevent them.

Prevention requires time and attention. It is not by magic but by regular interaction that preventative child development is accomplished.

Although the world of the child is potentially full of problems, those problems are not guaranteed. There is a gentler, more trouble-free world waiting if only we'll take child rearing seriously.

Read on!

BASICS

Never rush—when God made time, He made a lot of it.
Take time to be friendly—it's the road to happiness.
Take time to dance—it's the path to long life.
Take time to love and be loved—it's the privilege of the gods.
Take time to listen—for only through listening will you learn.
Take time to play—it's the secret of perpetual youth.
Take time to think—it's the source of power.
Take time to look around—the day is too short to be selfish.
Take time to read—it's the foundation of wisdom.
Take time to dream—it's hitching your wagon to a star.
Take time to work—it's the price of success.
Take time to laugh—it's the music of the soul.

—Irish prayer

1

Raising a Child

Never rush—when God made time,
He made a lot of it.

A wise old woman once told me that in life there are no free lunches. This is particularly true when it comes to raising your youngster. It's like a formula in physics—the outcome is directly related to the work effort.

Parents in general are interested in, and work at, raising their children. Sometimes they are impulsive or act on whims, but for the most part they share common goals when it comes to their kids. They want them to grow up happy, to be healthy, and to do well in school. These goals are high on the list. Next, they want them to have friends, to enjoy life, and to make them proud. Finally, parents want their children to find a good job, to have a nice home, and to start the process all over again. This can be a tall order.

"Experts" have strongly disagreed about child rearing for years. They have argued all at the same time that we should be permissive with our children, strict with them, and everything in between. At times, the majority of authorities favored permissiveness, while at other times the majority has preferred parental control. Although we have never been perfect at following their advice, we have tried, but we seem to be losing ground.

In truth, we were better at being strict than we were at being permissive. Children knew where they stood much more frequently when parents were strict than they did when parents became permissive. Children by nature respond to restrictions as long as they are fair, since restrictions imply caring. Children need to know that someone cares. On the other hand, permissiveness creates a feeling that the child is on his own. That's why permissiveness doesn't work—it breeds insecurity.

There is no question that in the past we were too strict. In many cases being strict meant being punitive. That's no good either, since punishment can destroy self-esteem.

The pendulum always seems to swing too far one way or the other. But during these swings we have learned some things that are critical to a child's learning and development, and which influence how she grows up and how well she does her growing up.

These rules apply to all:

1. There is no substitute for the right environment for learning. If you hang around with knowledgeable people you are likely to get smarter.

2. Learning is a life-style. It doesn't take *some* time, it occupies *all* time.

3. Discipline is not a dirty word. It is the key to learning.

4. Communication makes the world go around. Learn how to do it well and carefully.

5. Do not run away. No one else will raise your child for you.

Following these rules takes time, which is what many parents today have very little of. That means that you have to know what you're doing and use your time carefully.

Certainly the job of child rearing has been made more difficult by the absence of both parents from the home during the child's growing-up years. Although we view this as a phenomenon of the past ten or fifteen years, in truth mothers went to work during World War II and have never left the workplace. A smaller percentage of mothers worked outside the home twenty-five years ago, but the numbers were growing even then.

The impact of this trend on the business of child care has been intensified by other problems in our families, such as divorce and poverty.

There is another factor which contributes greatly toward the difficulties that we are experiencing in raising our children today. The changing attitudes that have occurred in our society toward responsibility, obligation, and commitment have created further problems that make the others worse.

Today's parents were raised in the sixties and seventies, and many do not think of responsibility in the same way their parents did. The loosening of the whole idea of responsibility flowed from the sixties to the eighties like a torrent as a direct result of the political and historical events of the era. Beginning with the Vietnam War and the aura of dishonesty that surrounded the times and continuing with the greed and duplicity of the eighties, the usual regard for authority was challenged. These changes had their impact on parents, who were often only obliquely interested in their children and found it impossible to offer them the direction or goals that they needed. Kids were urged to grow up and be adults before they completed the necessary apprenticeship of childhood and adolescence. Even professional advice urged us to be permissive, which, I have pointed out, can breed insecurity. It can also breed too much selfish concern.

Consider the impact of these changes in our classrooms and our homes. The swing was away from rules, discipline, and hard work. Public and private schools encouraged "open" classrooms, self-directed study, and a de-emphasis of basic skill development. This was a blueprint for disaster, and the disaster has happened.

In my office I often had a hard time telling who was the parent. Adults playing adults make enough mistakes; you can imagine what happens when children play adults.

Eventually, we as parents found out that there was no fairy godmother to assume our job. We have come back to the reality of child rearing, which is enjoyable hard work. By necessity we were forced back to the job. There are some simple rules to follow, and if you take the time to learn them and apply them wisely, the job gets easier all the time.

The job of gently encouraging the unfolding of a child's capabilities takes some doing. Parents find that it requires a commitment, some sacrifices, and a great deal of patience. The child has two needs: love and skills. But before addressing the needs of children let's look at the qualities parents must possess that enable them to interact effectively with their children.

1. Common sense

2. Respect

3. An understanding of limits

4. Timing

5. Honesty

6. Decisiveness

7. Discipline

8. Responsibility

9. Consistency

10. An understanding of the necessity for ongoing interaction

These qualities are not necessarily easy to acquire. It takes work to become an effective parent. It also takes work to believe in yourself. But if you're going to raise your child successfully, you must believe in yourself.

1. The first requirement for an effective parent is *common sense*. In any situation that involves your child give yourself the opportunity to step back, look at the situation, and ask yourself, "Does this make sense?" If you don't know, ask a friend.

One of the rituals of childhood for many youngsters is scouting. Usually parents are asked to supervise a group of eight or nine youngsters on some sort of excursion. When I was asked to help with an afternoon at a Red Sox baseball game I agreed, but asked the den leader if he had lost his mind. He assured me that hot dogs, Coke, and baseball were an American tradition that every young boy must experience. Our group of seven- and eight-year-olds was somewhat distractible and usually hungry. I knew these kids and I could predict their behavior at least ninety-nine out of a hundred times. They were going to spend most of their time, one at a time, jiggling to get to the men's room. While going there, they would pass the refreshment stand and argue for more food and Coke, which would start the men's room trip all over again. But no one believed me. I suggested that we tie a rope between each lad while going into the ball park so that at any moment by collecting the rope you would end up with eight boys. I was voted down. We arrived during the first inning with unfed, and therefore ravenous, youngsters whose sole preoccupation was food. I've always felt that baseball was dull, even for adults. I had logged enough hours at Little League to reinforce the idea that eight-year-olds can't focus on three innings of anything, never mind nine. We left at the third inning, but not until I had made four trips to the men's room. No common sense!

Common sense needs to be applied throughout many child-care situations. This begins with handling your newborn safely and includes everything in which the child is involved through the growing-up years.

Safety is a good case in point. When accidents occur in the home, a parent or caretaker may offer that he didn't think anything would happen or that he forgot that the gate was not closed. Children must be protected at first, then gradually be allowed to learn how to protect themselves. You don't want to make life a threatening experience for children, creating undue fears and anxieties about everyday happenings. But you have to exercise some common sense in their care.

It's sad that our society has so much available harm for children, but it's a fact of life, so we must look carefully at any situation in which a youngster, even for a moment, is left without direct supervision. We need to exercise judgment full time.

This judgment isn't limited to activities that are potentially dangerous, like crossing the street or playing with fire. It must be used in sports, social situations, and in learning. Common sense should be a part of decision making at home, in school, and at play.

When my girls were in kindergarten they were pretty good at ice skating for their age. I was asked if they could take lessons during the summer and work toward becoming competitive skaters. The first thought that entered my mind was that they hadn't yet learned to swim. The second thought was that the life of a child should have some breadth to it. It is no fun for a child if you rob her of her childhood. My answer was no. Other parents chose to allow their children the opportunity to take lessons for the summer.

Several parents spent endless hours, and in some cases years, at skating rinks as their youngsters jumped and twirled in quest of an elusive goal. In each situation I'm sure that the parent more times than the youngster hoped that this work would culminate in a major reward, perhaps a national championship.

This scenario has been repeated on ball fields, running tracks, and basketball courts many times over. Often the parents, not the kids, want the goal. Common sense gives way to some strong desire or unfulfilled wish of the parent.

I must acknowledge that some athletes in our society are very successful, at least monetarily, and that no one ever got there without lots of hard work. The emphasis here must be on the child and what is best for her development. Never sacrifice the child's need for learning by substituting for it that one-shot-in-a-million chance.

A wise old lady once told me, we all need book learning, but never forget common sense, because in life it pays off most of the time.

2. The second rule of thumb important to parents is that *respect begets respect.* Children are people no matter how young they are. They have names, feelings, and egos. Treat your child with respect and he'll return it to you a hundred fold.

How often do I hear parents complain that they get no respect from their children, who, following the lead of friends, run roughshod over them? Parents earn respect. They cannot demand it. Oh, you can demand it by force, but, in my experience, that kind of respect doesn't last very long.

Parents can also earn disrespect.

In my practice I care for a tender and demanding eleven-year-old, Alice, who always greets the office staff and me with a big hug. In the background is her mother, who is rough and verbally abusive to her. Alice would do anything to gain favor and a little bit of recognition from her mother. At the office we get to see all of Alice's good school projects and fine report cards. Her mother's response is, "Big deal! If I could only get her to pick up her room!"

Alice is hanging in there with her mother, at least for the time being. Maybe she will continue to do so, but there are many children out there who, alienated by a parent, have sought refuge in some unhealthy or dangerous situation.

Children build on love with a sense of security, self-esteem, and self-worth. They need to trust their parents and they need acceptance in everything they do just to reinforce that self-worth. They do not need unrealistic praise, but rather ongoing caring that is demonstrated and honest. Practicing this, the parent builds a bond between the child and himself that creates mutual respect. That respect must be built early and reinforced often. Once in place it will last forever.

It doesn't cost a thing to use your child's name, to be considerate, and to focus on the positive side. It's easy. Try it.

3. The third necessity is to set clear, well-defined *limits* for your child and to exercise some consistency in applying them. This is not very easy. There are a variety of forces that work against the parent in setting meaningful limits. The whole idea of limits takes discipline and follow-through. Sometimes the limits are suspended because it's to the parent's advantage to do so. This means that limits lack clearly defined edges.

Despite all of the problems involved in setting and maintaining limits, kids enjoy the security they offer. Kids like to know where they stand. Think about it for a minute: What do we do when we're unsure of a situation? We reaffirm limits. When a child learning to ride a bicycle falls, she rushes to her mother for reassurance before trying again. She wants to know that there's something she can depend upon. That's what limits do for a child. They define the space within which she works. She gets to know just how far she can push a situation before the consequences take effect. A teenager gets the same security from stated limits. That doesn't mean that the child won't test those walls to find out how firm they are. Reassurance comes from the confirmation of the limits, not the relaxation of them.

When I was in college I was asked to be a dorm master. At that time we had house rules about when you were supposed to be in your room during weeknights. One student asked about the rules. I responded that I expected him to show good judgment. I thought students, many of whom had been off to war, didn't need to be told about curfews. As long as no one heard them singing in the hallways upon returning, it was okay. He couldn't live with that kind of response. He needed to know the stated rules. I said, "If you press it, you might as well stay here on campus, for the rule is, be back in your dorm room for study by 8 P.M." He never could adjust to the relaxed rule. He wanted to change the real rules to something more reasonable. He spent a lot of time on campus.

Once I hired a research associate to work with me in my office. During the interview I explained that about one-third of the job was as stated and that the other two-thirds would be the result of his creativity. The result was a disaster. He was adrift most of the time doing not what I had in mind but, predictably, what he had in mind. We soon came to realize that he couldn't function this way. It made both of us unhappy. He wasn't doing what I wanted and, as a result, I was unhappy with his job performance, so we parted company. This was completely my fault. The first step in hiring someone for a job is to spell out what the job is.

You need to spell out the same expectations for a child: here's when you can play, here's how you come to dinner, or here's what's expected of homework. How you achieve those goals is what we'll talk about later on, but at least be clear about the goals.

If the youngster is expected to wash his hands before coming to the dinner table, as a general rule, but conditions modify the rules, then things are not going to go smoothly. If when Grandma comes you're serious about the rule and when you are rushing out to a movie you suspend it, then the child gets mixed messages. If the explanation was that clean hands are appropriate for health reasons, then he wonders why this is true only on certain occasions. The message must be clear if the rule is to stick.

4. Most parents I know have trouble with *timing*, the fourth quality that is critical for good child rearing. How often I hear the old refrain, "Not now!" Children are spontaneous animals and usually they can't wait to share a joy or an accomplishment or to complain about some real or imagined injustice.

It's true, particularly in today's world, that you can't be there for every exciting event, but those events remain just as important to your child. He wants you to hear about them as soon as possible. Plan on it. Ask him about his day or trip. You must learn how to keep tuned in so that you do listen and do respond. He needs to know that you care and that it's just as important to you as to him. Good listeners have good working arrangements with their children.

Your child also needs to learn when to talk and when to keep quiet. She must learn to be sensitive to a variety of situations at home, in school, or in life. How is she going to learn if she has no role model? She needs to learn to listen. She needs to learn to be appropriate. That's what timing is all about.

If by your actions you keep putting off that time to share concerns or happiness with your child, then the message is that you're too busy or don't care.

In my practice of medicine I knew a physician who talked to parents while standing at the door of the examining room. In truth, he spent a reasonable amount of time listening or guiding them, but by not sitting down with them he conveyed the message, "I'm too busy." My children, on the other hand, were seen by a physician who inquired about their school, their interests, and even their pets! He was saying, everything about you is important to me and I have plenty of time for you. I doubt if he spent much more time than my stand-up friend, but the effect was dramatically different.

Some kids are greeted with, "I'm tired, Johnny, get me later," while others are encouraged, "Sit here with me and tell me all about it."

Deal with situations as soon as possible, letting your child know that you're there for him. Kids don't want to discuss what's on their minds today, two weeks from now. They want to talk now.

Timing also extends into your willingness to discuss something that you and your youngster disagree upon. Find a quiet corner and listen to her point of view—not in front of the world, but just between the two of you.

There are many situations in your role as a parent where you alone have to make the decision. I have a rule of thumb: Try not to involve children in problems over which they have no control.

Always give yourself plenty of time to discuss or change something with your youngster before you run out of time. When you're on your way to the church, that's no time to complain about the wedding gown. Anticipate differences or problems and talk about them before they occur, not afterward.

5. *Honesty* is a critical element that encourages a good working arrangement between parent and child. Its short-term effect is that the child can trust you, and its long-term effect is that the youngster can believe in you. Children need role models in their lives, and you represent the first and the strongest role model for your child, unless you destroy the relationship.

It may be true that young children regard their parents as supermom or superdad, capable of doing all things. In time, however, a little reality takes over, and that's when honesty keeps that role model intact. Trust is the basis for security in children's lives. They need trust to learn and to establish the strength from which they can meet everyday demands.

When a parent asks her child, "Do you want to go to the store with me?" the child believes that there is a choice. What the parent means is, "We are going to the store." There is really no choice, since the child cannot stay at home alone. This subtle and unintentional dishonesty is confusing to the child. He needs to learn about choices and why you make them. A parent must consider the alternative and make sure it is acceptable before offering it to her child. Never ask your child if he wants a peanut butter sandwich when that is the only choice. Ask him how he wants his peanut butter, smooth or chunky.

Parents these days seem to have a mortal fear of saying to a child, "I can't afford that." Instead, when some unreasonable request is made they respond, "We'll see." I think they hope the child will forget the request, so they don't have to deal with it. Be straightforward. If buying very expensive sneakers is out of the question, say so. Children understand "I can't afford them." Give the child the alternative, clearly. "We'll go to the shoe outlet and find a pair that I can afford."

Children can't tolerate vague boundaries. They need clear, concise answers that are dependable. We all need authority figures in our lives, and this is particularly true of children. They turn to their parents for authority. If the parent can't be trusted, then trouble follows. As children grow they need a point of reference that is dependable, and honesty breeds this dependability. A child can be devastated if he finds out that his parent can't be trusted.

6. *Decisiveness* is next in this list of necessary characteristics for parents. Be authoritative, not wishy-washy. Some parents have conferences with their two- and three-year-olds to arrive at a decision by committee. Children like decisions with teeth in them. *Yes* and *no* are easy for them. *Maybe* is difficult.

Over the years we have found that parents' styles of child rearing fit into one of three types: autocratic, which means they are dictators; authoritative, which means they make decisions while considering everyone's point of view; or permissive, which means the child usually makes the decisions.

Authoritative parents are most effective because the child knows that someone cares, someone is listening, and someone is in charge. Security and direction are important to most kids.

Children make decisions like adults. Sometimes they have less information to work with, but the process is the same. Decisions in your home are the same as in business—they are made to benefit the decision maker. In business, your decisions influence your rewards on the job; the same thing applies at home. Children make decisions for some benefit. If the parent knows that, then her participation in decisions is made easier. She can guide her child toward correct decisions without argument.

Consider the ABC's of this process:

A. Get the child's *attention*.

B. Offer a *benefit*.

C. *Compare* what the child has now to what she must give up to get the benefit.

D. Make a *decision* to act.

The process is made easier if the parent is in tune with her youngster. Calling the youngster by name is enough to get her attention.

If the child is being called to lunch and she's hungry, the benefit is obvious. She likes what's being offered or she wants to satisfy her hunger. Comparison is made between getting lunch or continuing to play. In this situation, she may consider what's going to happen if she fails to respond to her mother.

Children are more straightforward than adults. Their benefits are needs or wants. Sometimes they just want to please. This makes dealing with them easy if you are clear, direct, and decisive. A simple *okay, no,* or *let's work it out* satisfies them. As a general rule, the simple, straightforward approach is most effective with children.

7. *Discipline,* often misunderstood, is one of the most important concepts in child rearing. Most people think of it as punishment, but the word means teaching or learning. Think of it this way: Children need to develop some order in their lives if they are to do things successfully. They cannot do this without discipline. The development of regulation in their lives is the basis for learning. When a parent is correcting her child she is instructing the youngster. The basis for discipline should be caring, a desire to help the child.

The idea of punishment which involves spanking or striking a child should never be entertained. It causes resentment and anger.

When I was growing up, it was fairly common for kids to be spanked as punishment in school as well as in the home. Many adults were in favor of this form of correction. There are a surprising number of parents even today who see nothing wrong with a "good spanking" for a child. I am quite opposed to spanking because it creates anger, not discipline. You should be teaching your child, not beating her.

Discipline is a critical factor in raising a child. It begins with discipline in the parent, which is why so many parents have trouble with the concept. The parents themselves are not disciplined. It is not easy to get a child to do a job correctly, because it usually takes some help and patience. Parents often lack the consistent follow-through that is demanded. This sends a message to the child that the job is not that important. Negative messages are received just as clearly as positive ones. Some parents want success without hard work and they encourage this attitude in their children. Unfortunately, success has a price. The price is called hard work. The development of abilities is a two-step procedure: knowing what to do and then doing it through practice.

The best examples of practice and discipline are found on the sports field, and our minds work the same way as our bodies. Our minds need the same attention to detail as our muscles. It is just as easy to encourage a lazy mind as it is flabby muscles.

Unfortunately, it's hard to recognize innate talent in un-disciplined people. There are many good athletes and fine students who never realize their capabilities because they lack the discipline to practice.

Discipline demands patience, understanding, and consistency. We must be willing to have order in our own lives if we demand the same of our children. I don't mean to be rigid, either with ourselves or the children, because that creates some unhealthy insecurity. Good habits are formed by gentle pressure, regularly applied.

8. *Responsibility* is the next attribute parents and children need to learn.

Responsibility is a very important part of child rearing, but it often gets left out of the picture these days. In the past, children were the responsibility of their parents under all circumstances. It was the parents' job to care for them, raise them, and get them started. Today, we've lost sight of this.

Some of those interested in child development a generation ago favored a more permissive style. They also suggested that you should rely heavily upon the advice of others when it came to the care of your child. That advice denied you the opportunity to work out solutions to problems on your own. Relying on others most of the time has a disastrous effect on parents. It robs them of the opportunity to make judgments about their children. It also robs them of confidence. It suggests that they are not capable of thinking things through. It's the same effect that occurs when a parent does a child's homework for him. The message is, "You are not capable."

Parents need to assume full responsibility for their children. They need to provide a role model as well as care in meeting their children's needs. Unless parents assume this responsibility, problems will cause them to look elsewhere for solutions. They need to be committed to their own actions. This causes them to think things through more carefully and put more effort into making decisions. How are the children to develop this quality in their lives if they cannot identify it in their parents?

It's easy for today's parents to defer decisions, even when the decisions involve their own children. Bear in mind that there is no one out there to do it for you. If the parent does not assume responsibility for his own children, then the job will not get done.

We see both sides of the picture in my office: some parents who are always working at their youngsters' development and others who abuse their children by neglect. Put first things first. *Responsibility* must be an important part of your life with your child. The time for encouraging skill development passes quickly. Missing that opportunity leaves the child without the basics necessary for a successful life.

There are no free lunches. You are the caretaker, provider, and teacher of your child. Work at it. Responsibility means sacrifice for most of us. Many parents must give up some of their wants to provide for their children's needs. That doesn't mean that you give up everything for your children. It does mean, however, that you assume a leadership role in the family. Children's needs, not wants, should be met.

I think that we begin to divorce ourselves from the care of kids around the age of three or four. Many parents give responsible care to infants and toddlers, and then a switch goes off and we think, "Let the school or someone else do the job." We may take our children shopping or to amusements, but we lose the dedicated attention and purpose that went into the first three years of life. We can't afford to do that. Children need us all the more after they are three or four, to help train them for life.

Parents should understand that children must participate in their family life by assuming jobs at home that need to be done. Children develop a sense of belonging and a sense of participation from helping. They also need the training that allows them to assume an increasingly independent role in the family structure. This is part of growing up.

Childhood should be regarded as an apprenticeship that lasts, for most, less than twenty years. During this time the child must build the foundation that is going to carry him through life.

Children need the opportunity to develop their abilities. This takes exposure and work. Our children's achievement is a national scandal and reflects inadequate exposure and work. Ironically, some of our schools' watered-down programs, which have led to this lack of exposure and work, are the result of too much parental influence in some cases and too little in others. During the sixties and seventies, parents concerned about school failure in their children influenced the quality and volume of work offered in the classroom. Some of the school systems around Boston show the influence of parental concern. Where parents care and become involved, the schools are good. Sadly, in other communities, a lack of interest is the rule, and the children's achievement suffers as a result. Schooling is also the responsibility of the parent. Some parents act as if their child's future is at stake while others act as if it doesn't matter.

9. *Consistency* in our lives is a quality that seems to elude even the best of us. Its importance in child rearing demands its inclusion in this list of critical parental qualities. Just because it is difficult is no excuse to ignore it.

Children derive a sense of stability and security from consistency. Most of the traits mentioned previously are directly dependent upon consistent behavior. How do we achieve consistency without rigidity? Keep things in perspective, listen carefully to your child, and always remain fair. Keep child rearing focused on the child rather than on others. Try to do what's best for the child at the moment.

Whenever we are tired, overworked, or out of time we lose consistency. That means that some good old-fashioned time management comes in handy once in a while.

10. Finally, good child rearing demands *interaction*. Encourage inquisitiveness in your child. Instruct the child to ask questions, to share experiences, to lift her sights, to think creatively, and to enjoy learning. Kids need constant exposure and constant feedback if that spark that is in them at two or three years of age is to be present at sixteen or eighteen. Parents can keep this joy of learning alive by encouraging their child through a sharing of life

experiences. Successful adults remember a parent who caused their talents to emerge. Those who have contributed greatly to our society rarely cite a professional opportunity that sparked their attainments. Impressed on their memories is the influence of home and the parent who insisted upon focused, critical thought.

Today, most parents lug their kids everywhere—to lunch, to work, to parties. Some do this out of pure necessity, but most by plan and desire. This is a step in the right direction. A child's life must be filled with experiences, and it's never too early to start. Remember that. Never deny your child the opportunity to learn. Keep the spirit of learning alive.

Due to hardships in today's world, we need to develop special strategies to address the needs of our children. Those strategies must include:

1. A responsible and informed child-care system that provides for the developmental needs as well as the physical support of the child.
2. The integration of day care into the workplace, allowing proximity of parent and child.
3. A revamping of medical care of the child, including instruction and information about child development within the physician's office as preventative medicine.
4. Recognition, support, and payment by insurance companies for child development guidance in the physician's office.
5. An expanded use of the public schools and facilities for early childhood learning and for ongoing child care.
6. Increased availability of information for professionals and parents on the developmental needs of children

Each of us working with our children can make the difference that will ensure them the chance we had at life.

We in the child-care professions have struggled over the past twenty-five years to find solutions to the deteriorating condition of our children. Suggestions have focused on improvements in teachers and in schools and on more federal support for education as well as for a wide variety of programs aimed at children. In many cases all of the above need to be done. However, the focus must be on the quality of the family and its influence on the child. That's the critical ingredient without which none of the above will work.

Remember this: Never let anyone else *educate* your child if you can help it. That's your obligation, your privilege, and your pleasure. Get the schools to develop her skills, but keep the process that establishes what she knows, what she believes, and how she uses her skills between her and her family.

Take the time to do the job of child-rearing properly. There is a time when you must develop your child's skills. Don't let that time pass without using the opportunity, but don't panic. Be purposefull.

Now, let us move from a focus on the parents' needs to the needs of the child that must be met if we are to insure the full development of his underlying abilities.

2

Speech, Verbalization, and Socialization

Take time to be friendly—it's the road to happiness.

Children are social animals who use speech to express what they want, what they need, and how they feel, and, perhaps most importantly, to interact, mix, or just get along with others in a group. Communication is a fundamental building block, along with motor development, upon which rest all of the other skills a child must acquire if he is to make the most of his natural capability and potential.

Speech, verbalization, and socialization—which reflect our ability to use verbal language, and the quality of that language, along with our capability to interact in group situations—are at the very heart of the child's world, as well as the adult's. The functions of language and socialization are intertwined so that one helps the other develop. Furthermore, other developmental capabilities, including emotional, physical, and intellectual skills, depend upon the language and socialization skills of the child. The very ability to communicate is based on these skills.

19

Communication means getting ideas across to others. It demands that I express what I mean and that you understand the message. This two-way street enables us to build upon individual relationships to learn to get along with others. We begin that process as an infant, with the parent and others in our family, and eventually we extend our reach to those in the society that surrounds us. This communication, or interaction with others, helps guide and develop certain emerging skills that influence the child's understanding of words and new concepts and helps form her way of thinking. For this reason I've chosen to talk about speech and socialization together.

Sometimes words are only partially important in getting an idea across. The environment or social setting in which they are spoken is equally as important.

Once I was at a medical meeting in Dublin, Ireland, and I listened in on a conversation about a problem between the government and the medical profession that would have an impact on the physicians' retirement program. Of course, all involved were interested and up on the latest happenings. The conversation I heard between two of the doctors consisted of a series of clipped comments, sighs, and nods. At times both nodded in my direction so as to include me in the conversation. This whole interaction occurred over five minutes, and although neither participant completed a sentence, never mind a thought, each understood the other perfectly. They could do this because they had a common understanding within their group.

Children learn very quickly to operate in a group, understand its rules, and operate within them. Just like those doctors were doing.

Recently I came across a fairly new book on child development that repeated the old belief that children from eighteen to twenty-four months engage in self-play and do not interact. By thirty-six months the children play side by side with other children in what we call parallel play, which is characterized by little or no interaction. At age four these same children engage in associative play, which involves others but not in a cooperative way. Finally, by five years they help one another. Now they are really playing!

That evening I sat in our kitchen and watched our eighteen-month-old grandson, who was visiting us for a few days, interact with our eight-month-old grandson, who is currently a permanent resident of our household. The eight-month-old sitting on the floor with a variety of toys would raise a toy to his approaching cousin, who might take it and walk away with it, soon to return with a substitute toy. The older child might also elect simply to put it on the floor next to the eight-month-old. Occasionally the eight-month-old would cry when a toy was taken. This crying would cause the eighteen-month-old to return the toy and then put his arms around the infant and his head on his lap for reassurance.

These children, along with two granddaughters in the family, one of whom is also eighteen months old, see a lot of each other and move in and out of one another's lives, playing and interacting with great regularity. Their interaction is quite meaningful and directed. Certainly parallel play occurs sometimes, but the majority of their play is with one another.

My wife and I are very used to this. We had "Irish triplets," twins with a third child born eleven months later, and often remarked on the quality of their interaction early in life. They played all sorts of games together and regularly occupied one another's time as they were growing up.

The point here is that children who are placed in social settings with other children of their age learn to adapt more quickly to the rules that allow group rather than individual behavior. Children learn to verbalize to each other very quickly, even if the words they use are not as perfect as they will be in the future. Gradually they will fit the words into the situation to improve the exchange of information.

Once our three oldest were with us in Montreal visiting a family in which the two children did not know English. They spoke French and German. The five children played successfully, settling in on German as the closest to English. Two of them knew no English and three knew no German, but they all understood the play situation very well.

I chose speech as the first skill to describe because usually it is the first function to mature in the growing child. To be sure, some youngsters are not good talkers and many go through life carefully choosing their words without ever developing good verbal skills. There is a wide variation in abilities across a group of children. I see eighteen-month-olds who say one or two words and two-year-olds who speak clearly in long, well-chosen sentences, sometimes better than many adults. The eighteen-month-old may actually understand a great deal of what he hears spoken and might respond in action to a wide variety of requests and questions without verbalizing much on his own. Talkative kids are prized (at first) by proud parents, and, in truth, teachers in school tend to view the articulate child as brighter. This may not be true, of course, since there are many youngsters who are very bright but not verbal. We in our society have always leaned toward the verbal child. The quality of a child's verbalization gives you an immediate indication of how clearly the youngster is thinking and how well he puts concepts together. With the nonverbal child you usually have to drag it out of him.

I once asked several children—some who verbalized very well and others who tended to be nonverbal—to solve a puzzle that demanded a particular use of a group of objects. Those who talked to themselves about the solution actually helped themselves arrive at a solution more quickly than those who did not verbalize. While verbalization facilitates problem solving in some instances, it does not mean that nonverbal children are less intelligent.

Speech and verbalization are the beginning of the child's language formation. This is a process that begins at the nursery door, unfolds throughout the child's developmental years, and continues well into adulthood.

The child begins this process by using words that arise out of his primitive babble. These early words that identify "Mama" or "Dada" or wants and needs are eventually linked together into groups that become the early sentences of the child's language. In time, these rudimentary words and sentences form the ideas that allow the child to think something through clearly and use words to express it.

Children normally turn their babble into words at around a year of age and the words into sentences at around two years of age. During these first few years children are usually bombarded with sounds and words by caring parents who are sometimes naming, sometimes instructing and at other times just carrying on conversation. Does the intensity of this parental effort add up to anything? Yes, it does. The better the quality of the language in the child's environment, the better the language of the child. The old saw, often heard from the mouths of well-meaning physicians to reassure the parent of a nonverbal child, "His brothers and sisters do the talking for him; he doesn't have to talk," is nonsense. If the environment of the child, includes good speech and verbalization, then he is more likely to speak better. However, you may simply have a nonverbal child who is never going to be a great talker no matter how conducive the environment.

The first step in the development of speech in your child is to talk to her right from the nursery and always start by using her name. That shows respect. Children are no different than adults. They like to hear their own names.

Remember, the first step in the decision-making process is to get the child's attention. If you are going to talk to your child, make sure that he knows that you have him in mind.

I was always impressed by a colleague who during medical school took the time to learn, remember, and use people's names. They loved it and responded like my friend was an old buddy. I made it a policy in my office, once I began practicing, that my staff and I would always use the child's first name and remember it. Some of the success that we have enjoyed in the practice has come from this habit. In our office building, kids who are there to see another doctor or dentist will just drop in sometimes because it's a friendly place, but mostly for some recognition.

Although children do not necessarily learn to talk by imitating adult speech, they certainly learn from it. They learn words and what they mean. They also learn how to use them, and in an increasingly correct and appropriate way. Often you'll note that children understand much more than they say. How often do we see a toddler who responds easily to various requests but says very little?

The lesson we must learn is that our everyday conversation with a youngster should be specific and clear.

Use words carefully and be very specific in word choice. Use the word *photographer* instead of calling him *the man over there with the camera*. When you introduce a new word that is appropriate for the child at his or her age, reinforce it. Use it again and then ask the child what we call a man with a camera.

Keep in mind that we all learn vocabulary best by encountering a word in context first, then by associating the new word with something we already know, and finally by practicing using the word correctly. You'll hear me say over and over that learning by experience, which is then associated to something we already know, and finally practiced, is the best way to learn new information.

If we read books on memory or attend one of those demonstrations on feats of memory, we find that the basis for the ability to remember a series of names is always association. Sometimes the person relates the name to something that stands out in your memory more easily. With a child you want to place each new word within some experience shared by the parent and child so it makes sense and will be more easily learned.

Use everyday situations at home, at the store, or on a walk to play word games with your child. Encourage her to name various objects in her immediate world to test her knowledge and to reinforce what you think she knows.

To get a child to remember the letters of the alphabet, try a song or a game that uses each letter to start the name of an animal or an object. This reinforces the letters so they are learned more quickly and then places them in a sequence, which again makes the task easier. This approach to learning the alphabet also gives each letter a sound, which is a critical step in the teaching of reading later on.

When you speak of a toy attach a color to it, if appropriate, like the *red ball*, associating and reinforcing the color *red*. As often as possible name the places you're going to and use names for the items encountered there. The supermarket is a wonderful place for teaching because it's filled with interesting shapes, colors, and foods, and also with groups like vegetables and fruits and dairy products. A trip to the supermarket also encourages the child to help with the shopping (and the putting away at home!). Shopping can also be a good learning exercise in appropriate social behavior. This is the time to establish some rules that limit how the child is to behave at the store, such as not reaching for every candy bar or cookie available. The store is also a place where one child can share certain responsibilities with a brother or sister by helping them participate in shopping or by helping the parents keep control.

To make a trip to the store for groceries a learning experience and not a battle, a little preparation and patience is needed. It is true that children make us less efficient than we would be alone and that they are also easily distracted. However, they have to learn like we all did. Begin the adventure by informing the child that you're headed for the store. Perhaps you should allow the child to help prepare a list of what's needed. You'll get much better cooperation if you take the time to allow him to realize that he is part of the project and has a job to accomplish. Make sure that you're prepared to take the time to offer help and that you're willing and able to exercise control. Don't make it an unpleasant experience.

There are three rules to follow when planning to use a trip to the supermarket as a learning experience: prepare yourself and the child, plan the time necessary to shop leisurely (since much more time is necessary when your child is along), and do what you said you were going to do. If it's to be an enjoyable learning experience, don't disappoint the child or she'll reject the opportunity the next time.

Children need preparation for new places and experiences. You must tell your child what he is going to see, where he is going, and when he is leaving. Once you get there, talk about it to make sure that he sees and experiences what's there. Finally, get the child to verbalize about the trip or the day on the way home and at the dinner table that evening. Your conversation on the way home helps reinforce immediate memory and demands some verbalization, while the dinner session gives you an idea of how much stuck.

Remember, never get a child excited too soon. Don't tell her about the trip to the science museum a week away. Children are instantaneous animals who operate more or less in the present. Keep the preparation time short and clear.

Once the trip or experience has occurred, relate present experiences, like the animal just seen or the bird perched on the feeder, to the one you had last week at the animal farm or museum. This is the association and reinforcement that will solidify the experience in the mind of the child.

Keep the questions and conversation flowing. Use your time with the child to question her, to get responses from her. It encourages her to use words, language, and concepts, and it gets her to think. This is what the trip was all about.

An awful lot of child verbalization is built upon a comfortable social situation within the family or with other children. The child's role changes depending upon the makeup of the social group and depending upon the expectations of those in the group.

One of my grandchildren is usually an energetic talker, chatting on in an animated fashion about things that we do or places she has visited, telling stories with great enthusiasm. However, with some members of the family who are not in our household, she becomes shy and reserved, with very little spontaneous speech. In a comfortable social setting, with children she knows, she can be downright bossy, letting everyone know precisely what they can and cannot do. Although this variation in behavior is not unusual, it is often frustrating to parents who want their child to shine in all situations, especially in school participation.

In directing the development of good verbalization skills, the parent needs to expand the child's social setting. Otherwise, verbalization will not continue to grow and mature, and the child will not feel comfortable about trying out the new words or language that he is acquiring.

Let me give you an example about a parent whose child I saw many years ago. This parent was a native-born German who had had a considerable background in English before being transferred to New York for work. Although he possessed a pretty good English vocabulary he wouldn't use it. He felt uncomfortable with the language even though he could ask directions and understand his children and fellow workers who spoke English. One day at work, during a meeting, he announced in German, "From this day on I speak English!" That's when his ability to use the English started and began to flourish. Children are the same—they don't have a language until they use it.

Comprehension of a language is tied directly to usage, and usage occurs in social settings. The best social setting for children is an active one where they interact informally and exchange ideas. Children need a response to confirm that what they have said has been understood and to keep in motion the flow of ideas that comes from the active exchange. This process begins with Mom or Dad, the initial sounding board for the child. Afterward, playmates and friends take over.

When parents ask their child questions they want to know that she understands. They want the child to think and then they want her to solve the problem or to respond appropriately. That's how children keep learning.

We were a family that enjoyed car trips, so we logged many miles in the station wagon with the five kids. During these trips we played word games, usually using the first out-of-state license plate spotted to set the game in motion. We would begin with say, "A" for Alaska, then quickly go around the group thinking of words that began with A. If an unfamiliar word came up one of us would demand that it be defined. We played many different word games, and they always made the trips pass quickly. These word games were not limited to road trips, though. We often played at the dinner table or at any other gathering where the family had some time on their hands.

Our dinner-time conversations were always lively, with everyone joining in to tell of the day's events or the goal scored on the sports field. Often we'd ask that a new word be brought to the table by each of the children to share with the others. Since an element of competition existed among the children, each wanted a word that the others would not have known. As they grew older, they found new words in books or on TV news.

Reading, which we'll discuss in more detail in a later chapter, is the child's ongoing exposure to new worlds and ideas. The whole process of learning to read starts at a young age, long before the child is expected to read himself. Children need to be exposed to stories and storytelling early. They begin to associate the pleasure of the story being read, the parental contact, and the information imparted as integral parts of their lives.

My wife ended each day with each child at bedtime by reading a story of his or her choice. This is a tradition that our children continue with their own children today, even with the eighteen-month-old youngsters. It's a very good habit to develop with your child, and it cannot begin too early.

There are plenty of good places to get terrific books, especially your local library, and you can take your children there on a regular basis. I usually comb bookstores and shops that sell children's books to keep a ready supply on hand as gifts for the children (grandchildren) and also to keep in my office or at home. Children love the stories and the pictures, they enjoy being read to, and, what's more important, they develop the habit of recognizing and expecting books as part of their lives. We're not only helping them to learn things from books, we're also establishing good habits and letting them know that the people they love value books and reading. Kids need good role models.

About fifteen years ago, after one of my postgraduate fellowships, I was asked to investigate how children from a small group of towns in southeastern Massachusetts learned. One of the things we did there was to find out how often parents of elementary school kids used the public library. Among the parents whose kids were doing poorly in school, an amazing 50 percent rarely used the library, and nearly 25 percent never used it at all. The public library is a parent's best friend because a considerable effort goes into providing programs, reading sessions, and quality materials to develop and support your child's reading ability. Those who ignore this advantage deny their child the opportunity for learning today and the habit of learning for tomorrow.

Getting a child to become a reader must begin early and be sustained by a good example.

Use your reading material to expose children to other cultures, differences in thought or behavior, and how we all depend upon others. Make reading time an opportunity to discuss new ideas. Keep a lively flow of information going, but make it go both ways. Be sure your youngster understands what is being read by asking him to repeat ideas in his own words.

One of the advantages of early exposure to reading is the opportunity to use books as a source of new ideas that can be discussed between parent and child. Furthermore, reading provides a chance to think out loud, to question, and solve problems. Reading encourages language use and offers a unique way for a child to extend her oral language ability.

Always take the time to insist that a child express himself clearly about some experience. Words are the tools of thinking and the child's access to words comes from talking about events or experiences and reading.

Oral language often reflects the quality of the child's thinking. Children exposed to learning experiences and urged to discuss those experiences and explain ideas have the chance to develop logical thinking.

The common feature that stands out in the lives of all creative people is a questioning parent who demanded that his or her children think things through and make sense of them.

A problem faced by many parents today is a limitation on the time they have to interact with their children. Involve your kids, talk to them, get them to verbalize. Always share and talk about experiences. Above all, use your time with them wisely.

Sometimes you'll find children like to use their hands more than their words. There's nothing wrong with that approach to learning. I've always been quick to urge parents to create an area in their home where children can use drawing or painting materials to think on paper. Usually children love to draw, and they'll go from drawing the basic shapes, to people, and finally to stories about people or the family. They will share these creative times with playmates and spend hours drawing or painting. Encourage this by getting the child to tell about her pictures. Give her the opportunity to show them off, to hang them up. Even let her give them away to special people like a favorite aunt (or a favorite grandfather!). It's a good strategy to designate a place at home—perhaps in the kitchen or in the child's room—where recent creations can be displayed. Every home should have a bulletin board in the kitchen for children's accomplishments and reminders.

Storytelling is another wonderful way for children to use language, and it is also a way to connect events and people into tales that are interesting and that make a particular point. Parents should use this strategy with their children to add interest and reinforcement to any lesson they wish to impart. Most children's tales that have been handed down to us are built around some moral issue to which children should be exposed.

It has even been argued that children's stories about dragons and witches are indeed appropriate for children to hear because they offer the parent the opportunity to expose the child to the issue of evil and to discuss it.

The heritage of storytelling among the Irish came from the absence of books and writing ability among the common people. From this heritage my grandmother developed the art of combining interesting stories and lessons. I had reason while raising our own children to use storytelling for entertainment as well as for lessons.

I began storytelling when our youngest child, at five, had a ski injury requiring increased time in bed. To him this was preferable to reading. Each evening I spent time telling stories that introduced familiar people and events. These tales allowed me the opportunity to get a lesson across while providing entertainment. They produced a lively exchange between us and gave him the chance to ask many questions. Soon the other children joined us for the nightly story. Their presence added to the quality of the sessions because their interaction allowed introduction of more complex reasoning.

This is what happens when a child uses a social setting to learn. Simple language is replaced by more sophisticated ideas and words take on new meaning. Concrete events become abstract and the child adds a dimension to his understanding that would not occur otherwise.

My grandmother's influence was put to good use.

It occurred to me that I was overlooking a good learning tool. To encourage storytelling, I found some tape recorders that the children could use to record their own stories, play them back, and improve upon them. This was a great way for them to use words and language, learn to keep a sensible flow to a story, and improve upon it until it was interesting enough to play for someone in the family. The kids loved it. I used to hear them in their bedrooms composing a story with three or four characters, each with a different voice, and enjoying every minute of it. The entire process improved both their speaking and listening skills.

Children, given the opportunity, will build upon their storytelling capabilities to introduce friends into play situations where stories are acted out. They will share ideas, interact with others, and jointly re-create life situations that need solutions.

Safety is an important step in the learning process for any child, and safety involves verbalization skills. It is hard to enforce good safety strategies within the home without developing the willingness within each child to verbalize information that may need to be passed on to some safety officer quickly and clearly. Parents must make their children familiar with the community and must teach them how to summon help in that community by calling a police officer or the fire department, for example.

Verbal skills, particularly in these situations, are interwoven with social skills. Children who are not socially experienced or sensitive often fail to read social signals correctly and may be paralyzed when some dangerous situation occurs.

Talking at home, then, has an important safety aspect as well as a learning one. A parent must assume this obligation early. It is the parent's obligation to instruct the child to be able to ask questions, seek help, and know how to get around. Equally as important, particularly these days, is teaching your child to know which places to avoid. The youngster who is able to verbalize is far safer in our society than the one who isn't. Children must know their phone numbers and addresses. It is dangerous to be unable to tell someone who is trying to help you what he needs to know.

The more you verbalize with your child, the more sensitive you become to what he needs to know and to what he should be learning.

While on the subject of verbalization, what do you do about the incorrectly pronounced words or the grammatical errors that occur in your child's speech? Should you let them slip by without notice?

The answer to this question is: use common sense. Never interrupt an enthusiastic storyteller and don't spend your life pouncing on grammatical errors. While children are growing up there will be plenty of opportunities to offer correction. Don't let the child develop habits of poor grammar or poor pronunciation, but do it without criticism and impatience.

If you just don't understand what the child is saying, get him to slow down and repeat it carefully. The child wants you to listen. Don't ignore the statement or story because you can't understand it. But be sure that corrections of pronunciation or grammar are always positive: "Say it this way..."

Parents are usually more tolerant of mispronunciations than are playmates. Children tend to help one another clarify their verbalization. Thus, another advantage of social settings is that they help mature the youngster's language.

Socialization has been forced upon many children because of the structure and needs of families today. Currently there is a much greater tendency for children to be exposed early to groups of children in day-care centers and in preschools. If these group settings are well structured, they can help in the verbalization as well as the socialization process. There have been demonstrated advantages for some children in day-care programs because of the quality and extent of the socialization in those programs.

Over the past twenty-five years we have learned that the speech and verbalization of the child, which are direct reflections of the child's language formation, are intimately entwined with the social development of the child. One feeds the other. Children use the social setting, through *interaction*, to build and strengthen their use and understanding of language. The sophistication of their language helps them to control and direct their social experiences.

These skills lay the foundation for other learning abilities. It is imperative that parents foster both verbalization and social skills in order to guide the emerging capabilities of their children.

3

Motor Development

Take time to dance—it's the path to long life.

Traditionally, motor development has been used as a yardstick to measure a child's maturation. The doctor follows the progress of the infant by noting her strength as she rolls over, sits unaided, or walks. As the child passes through the toddler years and begins school, the inquiring physician watches the child hop or skip, walk a straight line, manipulate the small muscles to pick up a coin or button her shirt. Why all this interest in muscular development?

Doctors began watching motor development to detect abnormalities in the maturation of those youngsters suspected of having some neurological injury that occurred before or at birth. It was possible to predict in some children later difficulties in learning as well as problems in development. These observations led doctors to associate minor developmental motor lags with delays in language-skill acquisition found in children with learning problems.

Although it had been known since the early 1900s that some children, despite adequate intelligence, learned slowly, it was the

34

emphasis on the handicapped child that emerged during the early 1960s that increased our awareness of differences among children's learning. This awareness caused the disciplines of education and pediatrics to focus on the motor system in an attempt to identify children with learning disabilities.

During the 1960s and 1970s, partially due to the unwillingness of physicians to accept the existence of learning problems, it seemed that every psychologist and special education teacher had turned into a neurologist looking for motor deficits to predict learning problems in children. There developed a whole school of thought that insisted children had to have a certain amount of motor ability, particularly fine motor ability, in order to read, write, and spell. There was even the school of thought that had kids (along with many tired and frustrated parents) crawling as an early step toward learning how to read and write. The reasoning was that if the child did not creep or crawl, his learning would be impaired, because children needed to pass through all the steps of normal development. But that reasoning is incorrect, since many children who are perfectly normal go from sitting to walking without ever going through the crawling stage.

Although motor deficits occur with greater frequency in children who have learning problems, there are also children with significant motor abnormalities who have normal learning ability.

One of my childhood acquaintances had significant problems with coordination due to cerebral palsy yet achieved high-honors work throughout school and college. This is not an isolated case.

The attention to motor development extended beyond the focus on diagnosis and became a regular part of the treatment of reading and learning disorders in our classrooms. Some of the children who were delayed in reading were also unable to hold a pencil correctly, copy geometric designs, or draw a straight line. Unfortunately, much time was wasted during the early school years with teaching these children fine motor skills, hoping that their reading abilities would improve. Although the training had a positive effect on their dexterity, it had no effect on their reading.

Similarly, it was claimed that these learning problems were the result of eye-muscle imbalance and elaborate exercises were prescribed to overcome the muscular weaknesses. Again to no avail.

In time, it was appreciated that motor delays were associated with learning problems, but were not the cause.

Much of this early focus on motor development was on disability, not ability.

But why are we so interested in motor development and why do I regard it as a fundamental building block in a child's development progress if too much emphasis has been placed on motor skills?

There is another side to motor skills that is critical to the development of a youngster. The motor system's development is directly involved in supporting other emerging functions in the growing child. These functions, all of which contribute to the success of the child, are:

- self-esteem;
- personal discipline;
- learning about the world;
- the development of concepts;
- general health;
- emotional health.

I want to explore some of the areas where motor ability plays an important role in development before guiding you through the steps you can follow to strengthen your child's abilities.

Perhaps the most important role of motor ability is one of promoting self-esteem. Think of the many situations where the youngster who is more capable at movement is perceived of as *better* or *smarter*. There is no particular relationship between walking early and being more successful later, for example, but the belief persists that the two are linked. Commonly, parents point with pride to the early walker, regarding this achievement as an indication of successes to come. The infant is rewarded for his ability by praise and demonstration to others.

There exists (and not so subtly) competition among parents of infants and toddlers for claim to the child who passes his motor milestones earliest. Conversely, the parents of the slow walker excuse the lack of ability in their child. This parental regard is translated into approval of the child and becomes a step in the development of self-worth.

The introduction of play activities to the preschooler at home or in child care regularly involves motor manipulation and the use of motor skills. Successful participation brings enjoyment and satisfaction. Withdrawal from the group, due to shyness or an unwillingness to play the game, sets the stage for loss of self-esteem. Participation in group activities has its effect on psychological as well as motor development. The process begins early.

Practice makes perfect. Good motor skills strengthen confidence in the child and add an element of social prestige when activities are accomplished skillfully. As child-care exercises lead to schoolyard games, and eventually sports, the psychological and social benefits to the child grow. This positive force in the developing child must be balanced, tempered, and kept in perspective.

It's to be remembered that some children are less skillful physically than others. Because of their limitations, they must not be judged inferior, nor should they be excluded from play. Conversely, the more able child should not be placed under pressure to lead play or win games. Neither parent nor child should emphasize this aspect of development to the exclusion of others.

A newsstand that I frequent is owned by a sports activist. He is convinced that children who play sports stay out of trouble. To his credit, he coaches Little League teams all year long. However, he leaves little time in the lives of his young athletes to pursue other interests. Excellence takes a lot of time, but balance and perspective are critical elements that the parent must supply.

Personal discipline is the next important ability that is molded and reinforced through the development of motor skills. Much of this begins in the child during the toddler years when the parent begins to ask that toys be kept in appropriate places and that clothing be properly stored.

Two- and three-year-old children should be introduced to routines at home—helping set the table for dinner or putting groceries away. Children enjoy the participation and the interaction. This is the best form of discipline because it establishes in the child a sense of accomplishment and a sense of order while learning. This kind of motor activity leads into other household chores and obligations within the family that are translated into lifetime abilities.

Motor ability gives rise to a feeling of success that is important to further development. If a child doesn't succeed immediately at various challenges he must learn to try again. Risk taking is a part of learning. It involves new activities not previously tried that require some problem solving. The child must think through certain motor activities and eventually he will enjoy success. These successes will lend support to his belief in himself.

General health begins with good motor development. The body is made up of muscles that are supposed to move, and movement is a critical element in physical as well as mental health. We can examine almost all of the major organ systems in the body, like the heart, the lungs, even the stomach, and relate movement and exercise to their health.

During the past year, we have experienced an increased focus on prevention in child care. One third of the children tested have elevated blood cholesterol, half the children are overweight, and 60 percent can't pass a standard exercise test. An increasing number of illnesses are related to poor health care, and health care is directly related to mental and intellectual health. Exercise is key to general health. Exercise begins as a habit developed through example and participation as soon as the child can walk. Studies in teenage children demonstrate difficulties reversing established habits of health abuse.

Mental health is another benefit of good motor development. Physical activity functions as a pressure valve for children in the same way that it does for adults. Once in good physical condition, your whole life program improves. Your routine is more efficient and your accomplishments increase. This is as true for the child as it is for the adult. Sharpened motor activity is reflected in many ways across the daily life of the child. Work effort improves, mental sharpness is enhanced, stamina gets better, and even social relationships are improved because of the reduction in fatigue that is associated with regular routines.

Although most research has identified advantages associated with exercise in adults only, a growing body of evidence supports the application of the same concerns in children. Because of the importance of developing good habits in the growing child, the breadth of influence of exercise in childhood for both mental and physical health is likely to be greater than for adults.

Poor motor ability in a youngster is usually associated with fatigue, increased weight, slow mental responses, and a certain amount of indifference that limits success in many learning situations.

There are social advantages to good motor activity. These come from two sources: the growing link between the use of play and games in a social setting and the social desirability of being well coordinated. Children's play, which has a strong motor aspect, is ordinarily with other children. Most games and sports are carried out with others. Children seek out playmates to share experiences which in time become an essential part of their lives. Sports become an important function of group interaction, and the success gained from participation encourages the child to use sports for enjoyment and group activities. This leads to the development of physical activity as the basis for social interaction.

Most of all, motor activity plays an integral part in a child's learning about his world.

Think about children and their early development, and immediately all sorts of motor activity spring to mind. From the very earliest movements of the newborn to the sometimes tentative actions of the preschooler, motor activity dominates the scene. The child is literally touching, feeling, bouncing off his environment, gaining all sorts of ideas, comparisons, textures, and concepts.

We have learned from developmental psychology that much of what a child learns from the nursery to adulthood comes from regular involvement with his environment. Much of that involvement is through motor activity. The child uses his motor abilities to confirm, reinforce, and extend his knowledge of his world, thus developing his understanding of how things work, and why.

Many children grow into adults who continue to use physical manipulation to solve problems. The development of motor skills is one of the critical bases upon which other abilities rest. For this reason, I judge motor development to be one of the fundamental processes in the evolution of the potential of the child. Without the development of good motor skills the child's interaction with his world falls short, limiting his ability to develop his potential.

Some parents worry a great deal about their child's motor ability. Sometimes this worry starts early, probably because of the not-so-subtle comparisons that one mother makes between her own child and the neighbor's child ("Oh, isn't your child walking yet?"). Keep in mind that many variables enter into physical development, not the least of which is opportunity.

I once did a study in the U.S. Virgin Islands of the learning abilities of several groups of children. Included in the study was an assessment of the children's motor capabilities. This was the era when we believed motor ability was a good source for predicting learning ability. One member of our team, using some standardized tests for motor development, found the kids to be quite deficient in some areas tested. I watched these kids move and play, and I couldn't believe the results. A week later we tried again, using an alternate set of tests, and the kids did superbly. As we examined the activities tested, we realized that these children lacked ordinary experience with some of the items on the test. The problem was that they lacked exposure, not ability.

This brings up the case of the infant who is put on the living-room floor and allowed to wander. When compared to the child who is confined to a playpen, the wandering child will crawl. The playpen child will sit or pull to a stand but may be slow to crawl or walk. Eventually both children will sit and walk. There is no known relationship between their early motor patterns and their language or intelligence.

Children need the opportunity to explore and engage their world. Let them experience all of the colorful things they encounter moving about the house. I am not, however, suggesting that they have access to anything that could even be considered harmful. Safety first!

Infants have an early fascination for black and white objects. Although some infants may take to bright colors in a few months, many remain attracted to black and white for some time. Hanging toys are good attention getters for most infants, as are books that have a smiling face, a mirror, and a handful of black and white images. On the other hand, never overstimulate the child by cluttering his environment. Keep it simple. Don't bewilder him. Let him focus.

Music and Motor Activity

Music plays an important role in our culture, and it offers a pathway through which many children refine motor ability. Parents can use music many ways to encourage the development of their children: as a learning tool, as part of play, as an accompaniment to movement. Music is a language with symbols and rules that transcends all languages.

The Hungarian composer Zoltán Kodály created a method of

music education to develop in young schoolchildren an appreciation of, and an ability in, music. His method takes into
consideration the developmental abilities (or limitations) of
children and has been adapted to the American culture by one of
his former students, Denise Bacon. Books such as Bacon's *Let's
Sing Together: Songs for 3, 4, and 5 Year Olds* and Lois Choksy's
The Kodály Method are available to help parents and teachers
begin the job of music education in children.

As is the case with any music education, the development of
rhythms gives the child a solid advantage. The Kodály program
builds upon movement, beat, and sequencing, and focuses on the
communication that goes on through music. When the producer
Steven Spielberg was trying to resolve the problem of communication between the aliens and the earthlings in *Close Encounters
of the Third Kind* he turned to Denise Bacon and her Kodály
program. Her hand signs, prominent in the teaching of the
Kodály method, were incorporated into the movie.

It has been suggested that children in Hungary who follow the
Kodály method read better, and sooner. In America, the claims
are that the children in the program have better auditory and
visual discrimination, better attention, and better sequencing.

Many argue the advantages of music in the environment of the
infant and toddler as a method for relaxation that improves
feeding and sleep. Conversely, loud jangling music stimulates the
child adversely.

Strategies to Enhance Motor Development

Although big muscles are the major area of development in
children under two, give the child the opportunity to work with
a spoon, then a fork, as soon as she seems willing to take a try at
eating by herself. You may need to clean up a little more often,
but that's how they learn.

From age two onward, children take to wheels. First there are
the little wagons or trucks, then trikes and scooters, and

eventually bikes. They all have their role in helping the child learn movement, balance, and dexterity, but each must be controlled since accidents do happen.

There are plenty of games and activities that interest the growing child and help in motor development.

The use of drawing/painting/coloring by a child is an important step that should be made available to all.

By three years of age most children will have an interest in using a pencil or crayons. Start by creating a space where a youngster can color or draw on her own and any mess created will not be of concern. Some kids need to wallow in their work; you don't want to establish an atmosphere of restriction when you're trying to get the child to be free. There are inexpensive materials that you can buy, crayons that are thick enough for the young hand to grasp, and books that are meant to be throw-aways after the coloring is completed. Don't be concerned about the quality of the pictures early on, just get kids involved. Despite the jumble of lines and seemingly unconnected scribbles, children often have very definite ideas in mind about their drawings. Remember that this can be a storytelling time for the youngster. There is always some meaning that lies behind the effort.

Give the child time to talk to you about what he has drawn, or tease out the story behind the picture. Show approval by displaying the child's favorites in some prominent spot in the kitchen, on a refrigerator, or in some area set aside just for that purpose. Children love to give their artwork to specific individuals, like an aunt or a grandparent, who may be represented in the drawing.

How much should you attempt to control these immature efforts? Not much. Some of the early awkwardness is a matter of muscle or nerve maturity and some a matter of overall perspective. You can help the child realize that one grip on the utensil may be more successful than another, but in general let the child enjoy his work. If you attempt too much instruction, the child will tire of the effort quickly and abandon the activity. As the child grows and matures it may become quite evident when a little help is desirable.

The next step along the line is painting, which will take more planning on the parent's part and maybe a bit more courage. Little hands generally produce spilled paints and messy surroundings. Prepare for this by setting up an area for just such activity. Easels to hold a pad of paper for painting can be purchased inexpensively or made without too much trouble. They often have racks where jars of paints and brushes can be safely stored. Keep a little bit of order to the activity. If it's too messy, you'll get disheartened and so will the child. Painting has to be enjoyable for the child or he won't get anything out of it.

Ultimately, the general exposure the child has to information through books, trips, or games will often show up in her drawings.

We seem to spend most of our school years trying to develop the left side of our brain, the side that controls speech and language, and very little time encouraging the development of the right side, which controls how we approach objects, pictures, or spatial relationships. Most of us think of sounds as the bulk of communication, yet visual or spatial relationships are just as important. As the old Chinese saying goes, One picture is worth a thousand words. There's just as much communication through movement or visually presented images as through verbal language.

Many visual signs, like those we see on our roadways, mean the same to people who speak any language. Similarly, hand or arm movements indicating eating or sleeping, for example, mean the same the world over, and are widely used to get a point across when you don't speak the same language as the person with whom you're trying to communicate.

Games to Enhance Motor Skills

Games can be a good source of entertainment, interaction, and learning for the growing child. Some games stress memory skills;

others stress good visual attention to details, like simple jigsaw puzzles. Still others allow social interaction through group play. In any game, however, don't get ahead of the child. If you have a twenty-piece puzzle that the child can do easily, move on. If, however, you're trying to get a four-year-old to do a one-hundred-piece puzzle, you'll have a difficult time. These activities help develop visual details, fine motor manipulation, and also some discipline to carefully build on small parts. Although there is wide variation among three- and four-year-olds when it comes to motor manipulative skills, and visual detail skills, remember that the squares, circles, and triangles become the letters of the alphabet. Once the child has mastered forms and shapes and begins to attach sounds to their letter symbols, the foundation for reading and writing is in place.

How about the major motor skills in children, like the ones necessary to ride a tricycle?

Major motor activity begins with the parent encouraging the toddler in play through running and jumping. Kids are quick to engage in activities in which they feel secure, and shy about activities that are new to them. Since they are rarely shy with a parent, you are the right mentor.

One of my children was shy during nursery school "exercises" so we found an appropriate audiotape and made a game of it at home. Once he was comfortable with the whole idea of running and skipping and jumping to music, the nursery-school sessions became a favorite activity.

A concern for safety is an integral part of all motor activities of children. Instruction should be incorporated into play activities to reinforce the correct way to participate without causing safety problems. Occasionally children get too enthusiastic and rough, and parents need to show them how to stay in control so that the fun doesn't turn into an unsafe situation.

It's a good lesson for a parent, too. He may roughhouse with a child and then suddenly expect that the child will stop without an argument. That situation can be confusing to a child who wants to know what has changed. Keep in control.

By three years of age children are ready to make the simple

strokes with a crayon or pencil that will lead to circles and straight lines. These strokes are used for the beginnings of the alphabet. Kids enjoy writing their own name first, if it's not too long or difficult. Perhaps half of those entering kindergarten can already print their names, and by the end of kindergarten almost all can. Learning the sequence and the formation of the ABC's is a readiness skill that a parent should try to teach the child during the year prior to the beginning of kindergarten. Note that I say *try*, not *push*. Some children will be slower and need help during that fifth year of life.

While a child is learning to write, teach him to hold a writing tool correctly, between the thumb and forefinger, resting on the middle finger. By four or five years of age, most kids have the manual dexterity to do this.

Although some schools believe that a form of printing (manuscript) is acceptable for writing, most still insist upon "cursive" writing. Cursive writing has but four strokes: circle left, circle right, stroke up, and stroke down. All letters are a variation of these four movements. There are some records and tapes made for children which set all of those movements to music. The music allows the child to enjoy himself while practicing cursive writing. It eliminates some of the boredom.

Electronics is an integral part of every child's life today. Children need to use some of the electronic machines to help them learn.

Should children learn to type? The answer is a definite yes, and some do a pretty good job at age five or six. In my experience working with learning-disabled children, who often have difficulty writing legibly, we always trained them to type. At least the teacher had a fighting chance of reading what they wrote. Today every child will or should be exposed to a computer. The keyboards are the same as the typewriter. The memory patterns necessary for touch-typing are more easily learned by the child, who usually enjoys the experience, than by the adult. It's never too early to familiarize a youngster with the new electronics.

They learn as quickly as if you were teaching them to turn off the lights. Don't let the opportunity pass you by.

While the topic of electronics is on the table, what about the large number of "learning games," or tapes and videos, that are available for children? Are they useful or not? What about Nintendo games and similar space-age video games? Without dismissing an entire industry with a stoke of the pen, I want to reiterate that the best learning comes from *interaction*. There needs to be some give and take between parent and child where questions, answers, thinking, and problem solving occur. I'd classify most video games as things to occupy time, not as learning tools. It's true, some kids gain some good hand-eye coordination playing the games. The downside is that many of these games occupy a lot of the child's valuable learning time and infringe on time that should be spent playing or reading.

Some of the toy companies have gone out of their way to create some first-rate toys, but there are many more that are useless or harmful. Sadly, we still see shelves stocked with all kinds of guns and rockets instead of with toys that would help children develop skills, interests, or knowledge. Jigsaw puzzles of the USA, for example, offer an entertaining opportunity to learn where the states are located.

Sports

Finally, let's talk about sports, or games, as distinct from play. I am distinguishing games from play in that there are rules associated with games that someone else has made up. In play the child creates his own rules to fit the situation. Sports, on the other hand, cover a wide variety of games and they have a more serious side. Someone is supposed to win. That's the object of the activity. Sometimes the emphasis on winning diminishes the learning advantage of the sport.

Sports for children can be healthy and constructive activities that interweave exercise, learning, sportsmanship, and discipline. Within reason, I believe all children should participate in a sport, but it must be kept in perspective.

Parents today are often too serious about their children's sports. Don't misunderstand me—I believe in healthy bodies. I also believe that good habits of exercise begin early and must be sustained, within balance. However, too much emphasis on winning puts pressure on the child and destroys the positive nature of the sport. Child rearing always demands some common sense.

Once I called a fellow physician, who apparently had been a mediocre college athlete, to talk about some issue in medicine. He informed me that he was training for a marathon seven hours a day. I asked him if he considered this excessive. I must admit I thought it bordered on lunacy. He didn't. Now, consider the parents who have their children spinning or twirling on ice at 6:00 A.M. each day for several hours at age six or seven, or the others who have their kids in the water for three hours or more, all in quest of some unlikely goal that I suspect is more for the parent than for the child. There are only so many hours in the day. Use them wisely!

First, children need to be children for a while and that means that they have time to play, ride their bikes, and do their lessons, so they'll know where Manitoba is. Second, young bones and the growth zones at the ends of the bones are not meant to be subjected to hours of physical stress before they are fully developed.

As a parent, take the time to expose your child to sports. Get him to swim (it will allow him to be confident, and safe, around water), or run, or ski, or skateboard, or even hit a ball into centerfield. Then give him the opportunity to define and refine those skills. Who knows, maybe there's another Babe Ruth walking by your side. But give him a chance to be a child, even if just for a while.

I remember the story Bob Feller told of his dad spending hours in the barn catching his son's fast ball until Bob threw a pitch (which he was able to do at speeds in excess of one hundred mph!) that nearly killed his father. His father knew he had a big leaguer on his hands and guided him in that direction. The point is that Bob wanted to pitch, and his father was just helping him fulfill a dream.

Motor development is an essential piece of normal child development and influences all aspects of the child's life. It is one of the critical building blocks and it creates a foundation that the child will call upon all of his life. It must be done with a proper balance, keeping in mind that it is something upon which other important skills rely. It is the whole, integrated child who becomes a successful adult, and any emphasis that places too much importance on one aspect of his development can be bad for the others.

Children need to keep moving to learn, to grow, and to be healthy, socially, mentally, and physically. But they need to keep a balance. It's the parents' job to see that balance is maintained.

4

Security and Risk

Take time to love and be loved
—it's the privilege of the gods.

Security is the food that fuels a child's capabilities and potential for success. Without security, the youngster will lack the willingness to take the regular risks associated with continued learning. Security is one of those essential elements in child rearing upon which much is dependent, and it takes a constant commitment on the part of the parent to establish and nurture it in the child.

During the past twenty years, many child-development experts came to believe that children form essential bonds with their primary caretaker (parent, grandparent, or babysitter) and that that "bonding" stays with them throughout life. Today, there is evidence that these bonds are less influential than originally thought, or at least that poor bonding can be reversed through strong parent or family interaction. However, there is no question that children depend upon a link between themselves and some adult whom they call upon whenever some new, strange, or threatening situation occurs. Kids, particularly very young ones, need familiarity in their world.

It is normal for infants at around six to nine months to react with displeasure when they encounter a new face. That's why infants who have begun to smile at their parents scream when someone new comes on the scene. The new person shouldn't take it personally. It's also true that the displeasure is directly related to the aggressiveness of the intruder. As is often the case, the new person wants to pick the child up, which intensifies the fright. Help the newcomer adjust by suggesting that he take a little time and patience. Go at it slowly. Let the infant get accustomed to the person.

This is advice that often must be given to family members who are not completely familiar to an infant, but are eager to hold or love the child. Frequently they pick up a screaming infant who is frightened by them.

There are other factors which influence the child's acceptance of unusual or unfamiliar events. If the newcomer is too loud or doesn't have a smiling face the child is less likely to accept the change in his surroundings. During the early months, soon after the child has really come to recognize a familiar face in Mom or Dad and all that is associated with it, there is a conscious rejection of anything unknown. There are children who demonstrate a perpetuation of this tendency to reject the new and the unknown, and this may persist for several years or longer.

Children, particularly infants, who experience illness or hospitalization may become unusually attached to a parent and resent the intrusion of any newcomer. This period of insecurity, often accompanied by crying when the parent leaves, can persist for weeks. The child might have experienced pain in the illness situation, or developed a fear of abandonment (this is the reason why most children's hospitals encourage the parent to stay with the child during brief hospitalization). This period of insecurity should be managed with reassurance and increased physical contact.

Bonding, attachment, and security are at this level more an issue of familiarity than affection or pleasure. Children get used to a variety of personalities in their caretakers rather than to a particular type of caretaker. It has been shown that the child can adapt without problem to several individuals who are part of his care.

In child care today there are many variations on the theme. Some who care for the child are just doing a job while others offer the same kind of attention and love that they would show to one of their own. In time the child will respond most favorably to the second type of personality.

There are many situations where a substitute caretaker has assumed the central focus of the child's security. This phenomenon has taken on special significance today when so many children are out of the home during long periods of each day while the parent is working. It is crucial that the working parent spend time reassuring the child that he'll be back and is not abandoning the youngster. If the parent establishes a routine that is maintained and provides loving support when he or she is with the child, the security of the youngster will not be threatened.

It is often more difficult for the parent to leave the child than it is for the youngster to be left in a day-care situation. Parents must keep a balance so the child does not adopt the disappointment or guilt felt by the parent. The focus must be on the child, and in this situation his needs must come before those of the parent.

At around two years of age many children show some reservation about newcomers in their environment. They have become more aware of different people and may feel comfortable only with immediate family. This is a normal step in socialization. Although parents get frustrated with their two-year-olds who will not mix, even with relatives, a little gentle persuasion without forcing the situation will overcome the shyness. Give the child time to warm up to the new situation or the new faces and encourage some activity or interest that will appeal to the child.

The same phenomenon can occur when children are entered into a nursery-school situation at this age. A little gentle urging, using other children and interesting activities, will dispel fears and initial shyness and get the youngster involved.

There are several major factors necessary for security in the child. The first of these is a central figure who assumes the role of a caretaker. The second is an environment, traditionally the family, in which the child ordinarily functions, which has structure, stability, and limits. The third factor is clearly demonstrated caring and love that flows from both the caretaker and the family that surrounds the child.

There are many opportunities for the child during the first two years of life to build upon some of the early security that has been established, or to accumulate fears that intensify insecurity. Some parents take situations that regularly occur with their child, like infections or exposure to "germs," in stride, exercising common sense and applying sensible solutions. Others get hysterical about any minor deviation from the norm. The calm, self-assured approach reinforces security, while the hysterical reaction breeds insecurity. For example, if a child throws a spoon on the floor during feeding time, a pretty common occurrence, all that is needed is a simple wipe and continuation of dinner. It does not require sterilization of the spoon. I don't suggest that the child eat dirt, but keep things in perspective.

If your child has a runny nose, and seems a little warm, step back and ask yourself, "Does he look sick?" If the answer is, "I can't tell," then you need a professional look. Develop some confidence about your child-care capabilities and give them a chance. Children respond to confidence with feelings of security.

The important thing to remember in this whole business of child security is that the major thrust comes from the family. Remember, however, that the daily caretaker of the child becomes part of the family, exerting significant influence on the child.

My childhood was lived in a small town where several rings of support existed. There was my immediate family surrounded by relatives who, in turn, were known by, and therefore supported by, the town. You could depend upon them and they would be there for you. I found this out because my mother died in childbirth when I was five and I spent much of the next five or six years in the care of the support system.

Such a support system has pluses and minuses. There is, on the plus side, a greater opportunity to expand the base for socialization, experience, and independence. On the other hand there was, as I recall, very little focus to the primary caretaker. My brother and I were the responsibility of maiden grandaunts. They had simple requirements for two active children: we were not allowed to rollerskate in the living room and they preferred that we not eat our lunches on the roof outside our bedroom windows over the side porch.

Throughout those years what I remember is that our aunts and the small legion of others who gave support to us taught us to believe in ourselves. This should be a prime concern of the parent and is a prime reason for the development of security in the child. Kids have to believe in their own capabilities to succeed.

Today we see a reenactment of that kind of support system for the children of parents who must depend upon others to do some caring and child rearing for them. Sometimes the system is less personally involved and sometimes it doesn't understand the extent of its role in providing security and learning for the child. These are areas where we must improve and where the parent must insist upon active intervention by the caretakers, not custodial care.

Caretakers must follow careful guidelines when interacting with children, in order to enhance their sense of security and emotional well-being.

Teach them self-respect.
Love them unconditionally.
Be sensitive to their concerns.
Give them independence as soon as it's earned.
See failure as a step toward success.
Teach them persistence.
Never try to be perfect.
Teach them to take risks.

To follow these guidelines the parent must connect with his child, offering time and understanding. Never assume the child's problem yourself; let him learn to resolve it on his own. Never criticize a child; disapprove of something done, but keep the focus on the event rather than on the child. Develop a sense of respect for the child through a healthy respect for yourself. Believe in yourself.

It is not unusual for me to speak to parents who have many self-doubts about their ability to do a good job raising their children. Their doubts cause them to rely too heavily upon others to solve problems or provide answers. You don't have to be perfect, but you must show confidence in managing your child or she'll sense the lack of decisiveness and this will be reflected in her own security. Children need to rely upon their parents as models.

The foundation of the child/parent relationship lies in the natural bond that arises during feeding, handling, and soothing of the infant. The child's initial relationship to the environment is created by various manifestations of hunger and discomfort. These give way to the pleasurable aspects of contact with his parents and the learning process is established.

Infancy is the parent's time for touching, hugging, and plenty of other physical contact to reinforce unconditional love for the child. This is the beginning of the trust and support that will build during the first few years of life. Physical contact is the key, and the child can't get too much of it.

Some parents think their baby is going to break if they handle him, or at least that's the way they act. Just hold the child firmly. Get in the habit of holding the child. There will be years ahead when what the child wants from the parent is a good solid hug, not talk or advice. This comfort is important to the evolution of security in the youngster.

As we have noted above, infants, once they establish purposeful smiling, begin recognizing primary caretakers, parents, and other members of the household. This period is followed by the "strange situation" phenomenon when an intrusion on their turf is met with a cry or some other indication of fright or displeasure. That's normal. This is a sensitive time for the parent, however, since many parents confirm the notion of fright by limiting exposure to others in the environment. Children need to know that life is not a series of threatening experiences.

Suppose you have a dog in the house that frightens the child. Should you separate the two from close contact? The answer is obvious: No, the two need to live together. (But keep your eye on the dog, who may get frightened or hit by an infant and respond with a nip. Some of the friendliest animals will inflict harm on a child when they are suddenly hurt. Be careful.) Introduce the dog gently to the child and continue to demonstrate that there is no harm associated with the animal. The familiarization process with adults, children, or strange places is the same and should be repeated over and over. The worst thing that you can do is to shield the child. Show comfort first, perhaps through a hug, then gradually offer exposure to whatever caused the concern.

Where does this fright come from? Usually, it is a direct hand-me-down from the parent.

Many parents, in their effort to protect the child, confirm danger rather than reassure security.

One-on-one interaction between the parent and the child, with plenty of new experiences, will broaden the child's exposure and get him used to change. It has been noted in cases where youngsters are introduced to new people that the attitude and style of the intruder greatly affects the child's acceptance of the new face on the scene. If the movement toward the child is slow and purposeful, without quick movements and with a smiling face, all will go well. If, on the other hand, the new person is aggressive in his behavior then you can bank on some screaming from the child.

As the child grows older it becomes even more important to allow interaction with other adults so that there is an increasing amount of exposure to adult role models. Generally, adults demonstrate acceptable behavior, so contact with them will strengthen your child's behavior and security in adult environments.

Some parents sanitize their children's world to prevent harm (to the child or to their belongings), which has a negative effect on the child by denying her access to the various experiences that are present in her environment. Kids need to explore, to try things on for size. Not only should you give them the opportunity, but you should also try to add interesting objects, colors, and toys to their world to attract their attention.

Common sense is very important at this stage. The child needs to learn, and needs to learn to experience control. Both conditions require a controlled freedom that strengthens security but allows risks.

This brings up the point of introducing controls on the behavior of the child that will keep you from spending too much time saying "Don't touch that!" The sooner you impose limits on your child, the easier it is to stop saying no and start dealing with the child from a positive perspective.

Often in my practice I meet parents who have active youngsters who push limits, testing their parents' reactions to various activities that they know are wrong. The parents of the testing child should respond quickly and firmly, making the limits of acceptable behavior immediately clear. If the parent's response is only a lukewarm "Don't" after several attempts by the youngster to elicit a response, this has two negative effects: it diminishes the child's security by its lack of clear direction; and it creates a pattern of behavior in the child that establishes misbehavior (especially for approaching schooldays) when control is desired. When behavior control, or worse, punishment, is imposed upon the child, he will assume that no one likes him. Limits mean security to the child.

The parent, through appropriate praise, reinforcement, and the eventual development of acceptance, will allow the security that has been started during the first months of life to build. Always show a willingness to participate in your child's activities and interests and show approval. This has the double effect of allowing some self-awareness in the child so that he responds favorably to his own accomplishments and helps to build his self-esteem.

Encourage responsibility in the child at whatever level is appropriate. Do not allow the child to assume complete control, but allow him to exercise increasing control over his own activities. Sometimes this is a big step for parents who cling to the notion that their child needs full support.

Eventually, parents have to rely upon their child's sense of responsibility, good judgment, and common sense to reinforce her own security. The child has to feel secure about herself and must call upon that security to deal with life situations safely. A child must develop independence if she is to function securely. To do this, she has to try new experiences. New experiences require some trial and error.

While encouraging some of these initial attempts at trial and error, help your child understand the quality of persistence. So what if he gets knocked down a few times? Teach him how to get up and try again. It is well known that children tolerate failure much better than older youngsters, teens, and adults. The expectations of children are different, too. They expect to win but it's no great problem if things don't work out. Never impose your own insecurities on your child's world.

An advantage to play is that it represents a place where a child can try, and fail, and try again. Children expect it and parents expect it.

A failure is a step toward success. Sometimes we have to try things dozens of times before the right solution is apparent to us. Remember the model of the tennis player or the golfer who spends literally years improving his ability to hit a ball. Unfortunately, that doesn't work so well when we place undue pressure on the activity and see it as a last-ditch stand. In truth, children tolerate failure much better than adults even on the sports field.

Children need to build some self-esteem. They need to be confident of their own chances to succeed. They don't need to be perfect and they don't need to carry their parents' failed dreams on their shoulders.

Throughout the developmental years a spiral of skills and capabilities helps the youngster activate his underlying potential. This spiral begins with parental love and caring, a response to needs, and interest in the child's activities. These in turn lead to approval, acceptance, praise, and encouragement, which create the three intertwining characteristics of self-awareness, self-regard, and self-esteem. This is what forms the security base that the child takes into successful teen years and adulthood.

Parents' respect for themselves and their belief in themselves are a critical factor in the development of respect for others and respect for their children. Without this, perhaps unwittingly, parents undermine their own children's security and success. More children have their security destroyed by their parents than fail to develop it at all.

Take your child by the hand, believe in him, and understand his problems, but don't solve them for him. Give him a chance to resolve his own difficulties.

Demand persistence and allow independence.

Be sensitive to her needs and listen carefully. Take time to offer comfort, never rush either her concerns nor your time to connect with her.

Above all teach her to believe in herself.

Without these strategies for interaction the security that you built in the child as an infant and toddler will not last.

And why do these things? Because you need to encourage her to take risks. Not in the negative sense of courting danger but in a positive sense of allowing learning.

In our medical heritage we view risk as the chance of something going wrong. We speak of the risk of infection or disease, and we view certain life-styles as associated with increased risk. I don't mean this kind of risk at all. I'm talking about the child's willingness to engage in some activity, not yet mastered, with a chance, perhaps a good one, of failure. The reason for such risk is to learn something or to accomplish some task that helps further enhance the child's abilities or knowledge.

One of my boys was skiing in the White Mountains and on a dare did a loop off a ski-jump run without any previous experience. The other boys daring him had considerable experience on that jump and were simply appealing to his pride (or foolishness). Fortunately, as he described the incident, he made the 360 degrees and a little bit more. It cost him a sore backside but not the broken back or worse that it might have. This is not my kind of risk.

During the period when this society became aware of the problems that some children have learning, we also became obsessed with the idea that children shouldn't fail. We adopted the idea that children don't fail; teachers do. In our efforts to correct some of the inappropriate behavior toward these children, we focused on the wrong area. Of course children fail— they need to. The statement that children should not fail is nonsense. Children need to fail in order to learn. Children should not be made to feel that their failures mean that they are not as good as the next person. They need to learn that failure is a step toward success. (The teachers also need to learn, in some cases, how to deal effectively with that failure.) Let us examine the statement that a child needs to fail.

There are some interesting things about failure, particularly where the failure concerns children. Kids are supposed to fail. In fact, parents are very tolerant of early failure because it doesn't matter to the child or to the parent. Whenever failure involves something that the parent considers important, the tolerance and anxiety change. In truth, all early failure is important to the child's learning.

If we do something successfully, we learn what we did right and remember so that we can do it again. In order to accomplish that, we must have had in place the capabilities to do whatever we did right or we wouldn't have been so successful. Consider the alternative, where the tools and path to success are unknowns.

The likelihood of success in this situation is probably slim. When we fail, a new set of circumstances is operating. That set of circumstances involves thinking time. Now we have to think! What did we do, why did we fail, or better still, what suppositions did we make that turned out to be false? What logical steps must be followed to arrive at an answer? In short, how can we learn from the failure and find the solution to the problem?

Still another situation faces the child as he goes about his projects that fail.

Children's early attempts and failures often involve the parent, and if there is an acceptance of failure, the child will simply try again. Maybe he'll modify something, but mostly he'll try in the same way. When the time comes to abandon the attempt, he'll do so without regret or concern. He's bored or distracted and something seems more interesting for the moment. He has learned something in his attempts, however. What he's learned becomes part of his problem-solving mechanisms for later on. As he gets older, some of his failures take on a greater sense of purpose or urgency to himself or a parent. Now this is serious!

Maybe the child has to accomplish something that is asked by a parent or caretaker. He's learned that there are different ways to approach problems, so he tries a few. Eventually he may fail at tasks that involve parental disappointment. Without the advantage of having experienced failures from early childhood, and the learning involved, he might quit on some of them for fear of the parental disappointment that he knows will follow. Children who are afraid to fail don't try.

Learning should always be pictured as a series of steps that are blended together so that there is no identifiable boundary. These steps are supported by security.

This is what risk taking is all about in the child. It's about the outward extension of learning. It imposes the real chance of failure, which has distinct advantages to the child. The only way failure is tolerated is through a belief in oneself and one's ability.

Skills evolve over time and they must be primed and fed by security in the youngster. The parent must keep this system going through his or her belief in the child and regular praise that reinforces that belief.

Show the youngster the trust that she has earned and encourage self-sufficiency and independence.

Show ongoing interest in your child's abilities and activities, and facilitate their development through support and *interaction*.

Develop a sense of family that will allow praise and approval from within the family.

Provide the time necessary to demonstrate interest, support, and understanding.

Make risk taking a habit that is built on a platform of tolerable failure and the exploration of alternative paths.

Above all, teach your child to believe in himself.

5

Listening and Remembering

Take time to listen—for only through listening will you learn.

Listening is a skill that is difficult to acquire. Good listening is an art form. Children need to listen if they are going to learn. Only through listening well will they be able to respond appropriately to all kinds of questions and instructions. They need to listen also, I might add, if they are going to stay out of trouble. For purposes of this discussion I'm going to include attention, sequencing, and memory as parts of the child's listening, for the three are interwoven.

The first step in learning anything is to pay attention to the information available. That first step is an all-important one. The clearer the information is in the first place the better it will be handled by the child's brain to make sure that the message is received, is understood, and is going to stick.

The child goes through several steps mentally to register and store information. Think of these steps as:

1. Attention
2. Ordering information
3. Comparison
4. Recognition
5. Storage
6. Retrieval

Let's take the steps one at a time, and I'll give some examples along with some helpful hints for dealing with your child.

Step 1. *Attention* in a child is raised by a whole host of stimuli which can be things that are familiar, noisy, different, or fearful. Things that sound pleasurable will also raise the attention of a child.

But what's the best way to get a child's attention? Call her by name. Children like to hear their names. Using their names reinforces the fact that they are important, and leaves no question as to whom you are speaking.

Make sure you follow through by insisting that the child respond. You need to sustain attention or the message will go unheeded.

Sometimes children respond to the introduction of change within their environment. Let me use the example of the sudden introduction of noise to a child in an otherwise quiet environment. Kids who are usually calm and peaceful quickly respond to a hand that is banged on a tabletop. All of a sudden their adrenaline flows. But what happens if the child is used to noise? You can get that child's attention by introducing silence. Try it. This change in the environment registers with the child, too. We get used to sameness in our environment. Any disruption in that sameness will catch the attention of the child. This can be a different voice, a different tone of voice, or an interesting message in the voice. Consider the softly spoken question: "Tom, would you like some ice cream?" Will Tom hear you? You bet!

Since one method is just as effective as the other, don't get into the habit of shouting. Be soft-spoken; it will get your child's attention without question. The child has to work to hear you. He'll pay attention.

This is a marvelous way to get attention I learned from the former U.S. Senator, John Pastore: I was at a noisy dinner meeting where Senator Pastore was the evening's speaker. When he began speaking, his voice became quieter and quieter. When everyone in the room was listening, having effectively focused their attention, he resumed a normal speaking voice.

To sustain the child's attention, speak clearly and simply. This way the youngster knows what you want or what you're saying.

Don't overload the child with too much information too soon. Some parents have a tendency to expand upon questions and, being unable to focus, the child stops listening to what the parent is saying.

There are kids who need everything handed to them one step at a time. If that's how you have to work with your child, do it that way. The important thing to remember is that no child will sit still while you tell him how to build a clock. If you want to say, "It's time for lunch," say so.

Stay with the situation, persevere, until you have achieved the desired result. Sometimes this takes a little reminder. Go to the child and touch him lightly on the shoulder, or look him in the face. Then repeat the message. Do so as often as it takes to get the message to register.

It is not a bad idea, particularly when dealing with a child who has trouble listening, to take his face in your hands and gently say what you have to. Ask if he understands and get him to repeat what you want done. After you have done this a few times, he'll pay attention. You're not chastising him, you're simply getting his attention.

Once you get a child to pay attention, then you move on to the next step.

Step 2. *Ordering information* means creating a natural order that is conventional or makes sense. Our numbers and our alphabet are conventional sequences. Doing something in a

regular progression, like going upstairs to take a bath, is a
sequence that makes sense and is easier to remember.

Sequencing clarifies information and makes it easier to deal
with. Some children have a great deal of trouble learning
sequences while others do it without a problem. The youngster
who has a learning problem finds this particularly difficult to
master, and it is a reflection of one of the many problems that
limit his ability to learn in the traditional educational environment. There are many youngsters who have no problems learning but who may need to be coaxed into the development of these
skills. Others come by it very naturally.

When I use the word *alphabet* you think of twenty-six letters.
That is one piece of information, so it's easy to remember. We
know the sequence. Listening is easier. If I present you with six
or eight random names or objects it's much more difficult to
remember them because in that case you have six or eight pieces
of information, not one.

Much of what a child does takes a sequence, some of which,
like the alphabet, becomes quite natural. Eventually we all need
to see that A comes before B which comes before C and so forth.
You need to turn the knob to open the door to go out the door.

Children can generally remember a sequence of events or a
series of commands to follow in a quantity that is one less than
their age. So the four-year-old remembers to go up the stairs,
wash his hands, and brush his teeth. The three-year-old will
remember only to go up the stairs and wash his hands. As is
always the case with the developing child, there can be wide
variation among different children.

I'm aware that many children go up the stairs and call back to
the parent, "What am I supposed to do?" This is permissible for
the three-year-old, but frustrating when it's done by a six-year-
old! But it happens.

The parent needs to introduce the concept of sequencing to
the child early. This can be done through the use of ordinary
household tasks.

Set up some of these tasks for the three- or four-year-old as he goes with you through your regular daily routine. Ordinarily children enjoy helping Mom or Dad do some of these routine activities. Kids are ready to help in the kitchen at three or four and will enthusiastically take on the job of setting three utensils at each place on the table or of learning how to prepare for bed by placing dirty clothes in a hamper, putting on pajamas, and brushing teeth.

Keep magnet letters or a felt board available in the kitchen or the bedroom to record tasks done. This will reinforce the sequence and demonstrate its completion.

When three jobs can be done successfully, add a fourth.

Rhymes, songs, and poems are good sequencing helpers. Memory games also can help your child to learn how to do things in order. Music is another good helper for the child. It introduces and reinforces a sequence that is pleasurable to hear, and, therefore, easier to remember.

Make trips to the park or a ride in the car an opportunity to sing a song or recite a poem to reinforce learning in a pleasurable situation. Use your ongoing interaction with your child to advantage, helping to develop skills while having a good time.

I've used the example of the trip to the grocery store as an opportunity to learn everything from names to colors to shapes to concepts. Don't let it end there. This is a time to put some sequencing skills together by allowing your child to help load the shopping cart. Once home, let your child participate in putting things away. This should be done in proper order. Each in order and each in its own place.

The better or quicker the child applies a sequence the easier it is to handle the information in the sequence as a single piece of information rather than as a set of complex pieces.

Another help to sequencing is to use the comics and separate the individual pictures or frames into parts. These can then be reassembled by the child into the original order. Then let the child create his own sequence of ideas telling another story by rearranging the frames to create a new sequence.

Use the evening meal as a time to talk with family members.

Ask your child to retell the events of the day in the order in which they occurred. Play the same game of getting the child to resequence events so that the day comes out differently.

There are some sequences today that seem to escape adults, yet they are easily learned by youngsters. In the past a radio had two dials, one for volume and one for selecting the station. Today homes don't just have radios, they have media centers. These regularly contain amplifiers, preamps, tuners, VCRs, compact disc players, tape players, turntables, TVs, and, of course, an array of switches to influence which speakers are to be turned on. Four-year-olds seem to have no trouble using one sequence of equipment over another for a favorite Disney videotape to be watched or a Mickey Mouse audiotape to be played. If the reward seems worth it, the sequence will be quickly learned.

The need for good sequencing skills never leaves the child. When youngsters are in school, during the early years, and even during the later years at upper school levels, the same sequencing is necessary to make learning easier, quicker, and more efficient.

There's nothing wrong with using some training in sequencing to reinforce the need to do daily chores in an eight-year-old, or to get a sixteen-year-old to pull his load around the house. When you initiate work to be accomplished by the children establish a routine that is clear and within the capabilities of the child involved. This reinforces the sequence. These chores are both a responsibility for being part of the family and an opportunity to learn something. Combine the learning experience with household needs and use one to strengthen the other.

Occasionally we see sequencing problems in adults. Sequencing problems are not limited to children. Sometimes in my office we encounter parents who can't do anything on time, on the right day, or in the right way. We give them the same instructions that we give to a parent for his child: make a list or a workboard with magnetic letters. List the work, the appointments, or the job to be done, and check it off just like the child.

When I was practicing pediatrics my wife often used to ask, "Why do you repeat your instructions to the parents so often and so slowly?" The reason was simple. Half of them would call me back to question what I had said as soon as they arrived home. Finally, I got smart. I wrote it down. Many people are not good listeners.

This brings up the point that it's hard to organize a child or teach him to get things into a good sequence when the parent has trouble doing the same. In that situation both need to learn.

Sequencing makes recognition easier, but there are other steps to follow. When the child has addressed the message being offered, he must compare the information to that already known, like a piece of a puzzle to see where it fits. He opens the storage bin to make a rapid mental survey to see if something there looks the same or fits.

Step 3 is *comparison*. Children need to relate new information to what they already know, and to find some similarities to help their memories and their listening. Parents teach this skill through the regular comparison of A to B. Draw the similarities for the child and show how A and B are alike. This way the child will know to seek comparisons to previously learned material and his understanding will be reinforced.

Regular experiences shared by parent and child broaden the world of the child, building an enlarging set of information, and preparing the child for comparisons that fortify listening and memory. Always discuss with your child how one experience is similar to another.

Step 4 combines the previous three steps into *recognition*. By the time the child has addressed what has been said, used some known sequence to simplify the material, and compared it to previously learned information, he is ready to recognize what's been said. Recognition also implies understanding, which reinforces the listening and learning experience. These four steps are critical to the next two steps, storage and retrieval.

Step 5. No information can be *stored* without understanding, and no information is readily available for use without comprehension.

Listening is critical to memory. The storage and use of information demand effective strategies for memory.

Sometimes children have trouble listening carefully, so understanding suffers. This is time for the use of a tape recorder to get the message straight, listen to it carefully, and then put it on paper. The reinforcement that comes from this technique can be a useful learning tool for children of all ages.

The best way to remember anything is to use both sides of your brain. We know that one side of your brain, the right, controls images and visual data. The other side, the left, is important to language and auditory information. If you use both sides effectively, you create a whole picture that you hear and visualize and that can be more easily remembered.

Important to the rapid and sustained memorization of information is the use of both areas of the brain to reinforce learning.

Most people use the technique of rehearsal as a strategy for remembering. Get the child to repeat the information, say it again, hear it again, see it again. The more reinforcement used, the greater the likelihood the information will be remembered. Rehearsal is an excellent way to "automate" some information. That is, make its retrieval automatic. There is a body of knowledge that each child must acquire that has to be over-learned. This information is then available to the child without her thinking about it. Obvious examples are the child's name, address, family members, and so forth. But the extent of this automated information expands through use. The greater the exposure of the child to experiences the stronger the base of overlearned information. There is, however, a constant flow of new information that every child must master.

Rehearsal or repetition helps, but association is the best helper of all.

If I want a child to learn about the events in Concord, Massachusetts, that set up the American Revolution, I'm better off if I take the child to Concord, walk around the town green, try a little Emerson on for style: "By the rude bridge that arched the flood, / Their flag to April's breeze unfurled, / Here once the embattled farmers stood, / And fired the shot heard round the world." Then the child can see the spot where the bridge once stood, head for Lexington, and end up in the North End of

Boston where the Old North Church stands with the lantern in its belfry. By the end of the excursion the child will have a much clearer idea of the minutemen of Concord and Lexington and all the rest of the players in those events. This is association, and it works. It's also what we call experiential learning.

If I give a child a list of eight or ten objects, tell him to read it over once, take back the list, and inform him that later I'll ask for the objects named, maybe he'll remember half of them, depending on his age. But suppose I get him to develop a story about these objects, making each item in the list easily remembered by getting him to create a silly or crazy situation for each of the objects that is "pictured" by the child's mind as well as "heard." For instance, suppose a ribbon, a hat, a flower, a mule, and a car were all on the list. I'd put the flowers on the mule's nose, that hat on its head with a yellow ribbon on it, and prop the mule in the back seat of a convertible. Do you think the child would remember those items more easily? You bet he would. This use of vivid association among the objects to be remembered is the first memory helper.

A second step that I'd offer to the child to help his memory is to group items that naturally belong together, like a ribbon, a hat, and a flower.

Third, I'd get the child, once he was comfortable and had developed some skill at the above associations, to create a mental image like a swan for the letter S and think of the swan as soft flowing music. For each letter of the alphabet I'd get some associations going that left the child with a good mental image. Now the letter, the first of the word or object to be remembered, would be linked to the mental image.

These mental images and associations can become games to play again at meal times, on trips, or during a walk to town. They strengthen memory and let the child have some enjoy doing it.

Step 6. The last item on our list of skills that comprise listening activities is *retrieval.* Helping a child to learn how to recover information quickly is a simple matter of creating an

orderly closet in his brain. A child needs to use his head
regularly if he is going to have an efficient system for remembering things that he knows or should know.

Think of your child's brain as a muscle that needs to be used
all of the time. It's an information center where there is, or
should be, a constant flow in and out. The brain's job is to take
in new information, add it to the information that is already
there, and bring it back out as needed. This is a dynamic system
that demands ongoing exchange. Brains need to interact. People
need to interact. There are many games that appeal to children
that exercise the brain and reinforce learning.

Grandma's Trunk is a game that requires memory and association by linking A is for apple, B is for boat, C is for car, and so
forth. It increases the speed of the child's thinking and calls
upon quick recall under pressure. Concentration is another
useful group game to challenge the wits and memory. Perhaps the
best thinking game of all is chess since it demands thinking
through your own steps while solving the problem of your
opponent's anticipated moves.

There are some key points that should be kept in mind as you
develop listening skills in your child:

1. Use your child's name—it makes him realize that you're
   talking to him and that you care.

2. Follow through, not only to make sure that the message
   was received but that the child is going to react to it. Too
   often parents are not consistent in their attention-seeking
   activities with their children. Habits are formed by consistent action.

3. Use a quiet gentle approach to your child that is firm, not
   hysterical—this promotes an evenness in your authority
   that produces results.

4. Take the time to introduce a physical side to your listening
   training. This can be a gentle touch or a more insistent
   willingness to take the child by the hand and lead him to
   whatever you have in mind.

5. Keep responsibility with consequences firmly on the child's shoulder. Once you know that the child heard you, then you can improve the situation by having the child's response dictate what happens next. Under the circumstances the consequences are of his doing, not yours.

   Even the youngest child can begin to take charge if the parent will get the whole message across.

6. Reduce the noise level so that the child can hear and respond to your wishes. When you have something to say, get the area quiet first, then talk.

   If you get the child's attention, the next step is to help the information sink in, to help the child understand.

7. Speak clearly.

8. Speak simply—the simpler the message the better it will be received.

9. Group together information that belongs together.

10. Teach sequencing. Encourage the child to carry out information in a logical order. Start off simply and move up as the traffic will allow.

11. Use experiences to reinforce learning. Create excursions to introduce and underscore learning.

12. Encourage associations that enhance memory. Use games and playtime to develop these skills. They take time to emerge and need plenty of practice.

The importance of good listening skills should be apparent to us all. Your willingness to start early with your child and apply some time and work in this area will pay off handsomely.

It's very difficult for a child to function properly through the growing-up years without good listening. It's also very hard to function as an adult without these listening skills.

Listening stabilizes and enforces memory and is the path to comprehension. It facilitates more learning and problem-solving capabilities. That is the need and the goal of enhancing listening skills.

6

Play and Learning

Take time to play—it's the secret of perpetual youth.

Childhood is all about play. Without play kids don't grow. It is the activity through which the child, using elementary skills, sets into motion early development.

Let me list some of the things that children learn from play:

- How things work in their world.
- What can and cannot be done with various objects.
- Why certain things don't work.
- All about success and failure.
- The rules of play.
- How to get along with others.

Eventually the child also learns:

- to exercise;
- to enjoy himself;
- to deal with problems;

- to trust—first his parents, then others;
- to socialize;
- to develop his language;
- to grow intellectually;
- to stick to a job;
- to keep trying;
- to work with others.

As you can see, the advantages of play are almost endless. And play is what childhood is all about.

For one reason or another we seem to regard play in a negative sense. We regard it as the casual, time-wasting activities of children. It doesn't seem to add up to anything but fun. We even use the term "child's play" when referring to some "adult" activity that we don't consider serious.

I define play as both the unstructured and structured activities in which children engage, activities that have no formal rules. The rules in play are made up as the child goes along.

However, when you think about it for a while, you realize that play always has an aspect of the real world superimposed upon it, particularly when play occurs in a group. If children are playing together and one of them keeps making up rules which are unacceptable to the others, then the play changes. The others quickly become uninterested in play that doesn't meet their needs. This is as true for adult life as it is for child's play. Included in this definition of play are the daydreaming, fantasy, and make-believe that all of us, at some time, include in our ongoing mental activity.

On the other hand, games are activities in which older children and adults participate. Games are formal, have set rules, and have set objectives. Most importantly, games have winners and losers—the object of a game is to win.

Some would argue that many games are played for the enjoyment of participation, or the socializing involved. The coach of the Saturday morning soccer game may console his team that the playing is important, not the winning. But he knows, and his team knows, that they step on the field to win the contest. The coach teaches rules and plays to the team so that they can play effectively. The object is to score goals and to prevent the opposition from scoring. Kids are disappointed if they don't win. Play is not only a forerunner, but a necessary antecedent to games. It provides the experience that allows perspective and coping.

In early infancy steps are taken by the child in preparation for play. They represent an orderly progression of activity that leads to play.

From the very start children respond to their early interactions with their parents. It begins with arousal, knowing someone is there holding them. This gives way to the pleasurable aspects of face recognition, the warmth of being held and cuddled, and the early give-and-take with parents or caretakers which is the critical step in the formation of security in the child.

From six or eight months of age children develop a sense of familiarity or belonging to the world that surrounds them. They develop an important sense of security about this familiar world. Children by this time know the faces around them and respond with appropriate smiles to those faces. Their sense of security fades rapidly when anything disrupts their world, whether by sight or by sound.

When a parent imitates play activities, the child enjoys the give-and-take because it fosters his feeling of security in his immediate world. Objects or faces hidden momentarily in play reinforce this security when they return. The child knows that something important to him is not lost or gone.

The simple activity of manipulating a rattle or a favorite toy gives information about shapes and weights that is an important step toward filling in details about objects within his immediate vision. This kind of manipulation reinforces and adds to the child's data bank of information and helps the child learn about things in her world.

Children imitate the actions they observe around them. Some of these are visual while other are auditory. In the beginning most of these imitations are of activities that go on between parent and child, but soon they involve others in the child's broadening world. These pleasurable activities become play. The child likes the response his imitation elicits from the adult, so he willingly joins in.

Play also teaches the child about control. He finds out that he is in control of the situation by his manipulating a toy or throwing it. He learns that no matter how often he does this, it is retrieved by another child or a parent. Sometimes the repetitive action of throwing a toy and expecting it to be retrieved is not done to annoy the parent nor is it done just for fun. It is done to reinforce and reassure the child that his possessions belong to him. No matter how often he discards the toy it somehow gets back to him. They child views his toys as extensions of himself. It is important for him to know that he can't lose them.

One of the hard things for parents to understand about a child is the start-and-stop quality of her interaction. This exists for good reason. At times the youngster needs to be on her own to explore and learn what's under her own control and not the parent's, to gain a sense of independence.

There are great differences among children, particularly during the early months when motor abilities can vary significantly. These differences show up in the character of the interactive sessions with the parent or the child's regular caretaker. Infants exposed to open and interesting spaces will often move around much sooner than others who are in a more restricted environment. It's important during these early months to handle and show love to the baby, to be playful, laugh, and show happiness. It's also important to maintain a stimulating environment in which the child can always be learning. The youngster will copy adult behavior. Start to experiment with simple toys and motions. Add more complex activities as time goes on and as the child shows readiness to accept the advanced learning. The joy, surprise, and happiness of this stage cements some of the security that will later allow the baby to engage in the social games that further development.

We learned from Jean Piaget, the Swiss psychologist, that there are three periods in a child's life that define his emerging play. The three stages that Piaget proposes are: (1) the sensory motor stage, which includes the period of the child's early contact with the world around himself; (2) the symbolic stage, or pretend play, which according to Piaget forms the second level of play from the second to third year of life to about age six (during this period much of the child's play is made up by the youngster according to his own rules); and (3) the cognitive stage, or the thinking period of play, when games with rules are first seen in the child's play activity. From observations of large numbers of children we realize that there can be significant differences among children when these periods occur. The labels of periods of play only help us to define and when and how children respond in a developing pattern and use their experiences to build a more solid physical and emotional self. The process that builds from simple contact with the world, through fantasy and pretend play, to more adult games with rules has immediate as well as long-term effects on the emotional and physical development of the child.

All children are a blend of the physical abilities they are born with, their personalities, which come from a mixture of inborn tendencies and responses to their environments, the goals of the parents/caretakers, and, finally, the environments in which they are reared. Play is a critical tool the youngster uses to engage in a constant series of experiences with his world that foster learning and insure his development. In some instances the child uses play to resolve differences or conflicts, while in others she uses it to establish and reinforce learning.

Consider the differences created by two parents whose goal is the same, to help their children fulfill their abilities, but whose signals and approaches used to accomplish this goal are very different. Although the examples I use are extreme, these two personalities exist.

One parent cares how the child feels while the other cares for what the child accomplishes. The first parent is tender, loving, and affectionate, nurturing the child in all aspects possible. She rejoices in every move, constantly underscoring the simplest achievement as a major event in the life of the child. This parent's excessive attention to the child will create in the youngster a feeling of less security and may even diminish some of the advantage of what could be a good play experience. The increased attention and intimacy between parent and child may deny the youngster the independence and opportunity for trial and error that leads to success. Children acquire self-confidence through repeated life experiences that they must in some way control by themselves. The child needs to succeed or fail and she needs realistic accomplishment. Only through this will self-esteem flourish and native ability emerge.

The second parent, bent on achievement as a goal, may establish standards for the child that are unrealistic and too demanding. Approval may only be offered for goals achieved, not for good tries along the way. This approach, although well intentioned, deprives the child of the nurturing needed so he can keep trying until the goal is achieved. The parent, fearful of robbing the child of autonomy or individualization by supporting him along the way, may create self-doubt in the child. Things don't always turn out right, no matter how hard we try.

One of the youngsters in my practice worked three years at a sport, setting a goal that would insure the desired championship. In three years the goal was achieved, but the championship was not—two other athletes were better. Children and parents need to appreciate that trying alone doesn't insure success.

This is particularly true for the child learning a new skill or putting a new one to work. If the parent focuses on achievement alone, instead of instilling a sense of accomplishment in hard work, he may well create a sense of failure in the child, who will see herself as disappointing the parent if the final goal cannot be attained.

Of course, as we raise our children we want a balance of the two personalities, one that offers constant love and support and the other that demands hard work, discipline, and accomplishment. Sometimes it's hard to achieve a balance between the two. Parents are usually in one camp or the other. It is important to appreciate that the content of the child's play is what is most important, not some end product of the play. This content has a direct influence on how the child develops the skills that are critical to the fulfillment of his potential.

The greater the opportunity for social play, particularly during these early phases in the child's life, the quicker she'll move toward more mature behavior. Many professionals believe that kids do not engage in active social exchange with other children until they are approaching the kindergarten years. As I have noted previously, my two grandsons, ages eight months and eighteen months, interact with the purpose and sociability thought reserved for four-year-olds. They exchange toys and respond to occasional tears caused by lapses in generosity by offering support or consolation.

Observation of children in larger families reveals regular social engagement held to be premature by some child specialists. The social behavior is mixed with self-centered activities and parallel play. This observed precocity reinforces the idea that the quality and makeup of the child's environment dictates the maturation of skills in children.

Many children in our society are in child-care situations early, and this trend is growing. In some of these cases, particularly where the quality of the home environment is wanting, the opportunity is present to add to or extend normal social development and to insure a better outcome in the children.

By the toddler years children need to make sense out of their environment, and there are lots of issues or conflicts that need to be resolved. Children use play to work out many ordinary life situations that in some instances produce anxiety. Children may demonstrate a tendency to be abrupt or impulsive and through reflection and play can modify this behavior. Various life events that provoke anger or are uncomfortable can be adequately handled by play situations.

Sometimes the toys, blankets, or cuddly playthings that were part of infancy persist as symbols of parent, parent love, and security that are not so easily shed. In some cases these objects are manipulated in a play situation by the child to offset, learn about, and accept parental control.

Fantasy is important in the developing child as a way to resolve real-life situations. Often, imaginary friends are created out of dolls or stuffed animals. These "companions" are frequent in the preschool child, but their existence for some children persists into school and life. In these instances the playmates in imaginary worlds, which become quite real to some children, help bridge gaps and indeed bring reality into focus rather than emphasize the make-believe.

During this same period play helps children in both direct and indirect ways with their language development. Again, we see broad differences in developmental timetables with some young-sters using a reasonably mature form of language around two years while others are just beginning to speak. Play offers the opportunity for social exchange, sometimes with the child alone and at other times with playmates. Objects need names and actions. Situations demand verbal activity. There is a unique feedback system between social activity and language develop-ment. You need one to help the other. If you observe children at play it's apparent that socialization stimulates verbalization and places demands on the maturity of the child. In like manner the more mature the language, the more mature the play activities become. Although I place great emphasis on language as the central point in development, it is intertwined with social skills in a unique fashion.

Let us look at language for a moment, since it is so important to the development of the child. Language is a system for exchanging ideas and as such it takes on many forms. For instance, math, music, art, and even our street signs are language systems. A language must have a set of symbols (the alphabet for us in English), a group of words (our vocabulary), and a set of rules (our grammar) that tell us how to combine the words into sentences. A sentence is a group of words that makes sense as an idea. We also know that sounds play an important role in making sense out of the string of words that we call a sentence. If the words can't be comprehended, then you don't have a language.

Play leads us to communicate.

How does it do this?

Young children, by playing games with parents, develop a group of words, each of which has a meaning to them. This becomes their vocabulary. They use these words to name objects and form sentences. No matter how simple these sentences are they tie one action to another. These early sentences eventually become more elaborate and descriptive, telling more and more about the thing being described.

First, kids learn that an apple is a red fruit that grows on a tree. Then they learn that the apple can be a symbol or a sign for a whole class of things that can be eaten, food. Eventually this symbol, the apple, takes on a more sophisticated idea that is more abstract. It becomes a symbol for the desires or temptations of life.

Through play activities that occur at home or outside with friends, children eventually develop a mental sense of what is being represented through play. They make up ideas or think through stories that describe life situations. They learn how to think through and solve problems. In time, through play interaction, their ideas expand and become less concrete, or more abstract. They begin to see that the ideas they involve in their play can be applied to a series of situations rather than just to a specific situation. In doing this the youngster transforms his thinking from something that is concrete to something that is abstract. Concrete thoughts usually express concern about the person himself, while abstract ideas usually focus on others. It is characteristic of the younger child to think about himself and of the more adult child to think about others. The child's use of words passes through these same stages—from using the word *apple* to describe a red piece of fruit to using it to describe something abstract that represents an idea.

We've learned that the more imaginative or unstructured play is, the more verbal, creative, and bright children can become.

The more you fiddle with a child's play, controlling or contriving games, the less interested the child becomes in life situations.

Imaginative play needs to have some organization or the activity, if it involves other children, won't last. The other kids won't play unless there is some sense of reality to the game. In these instances the leader needs to devise and verbalize an activity, no matter how make-believe, that other children can relate to.

Social and pretend play also mature the child's ability to use speech or language more quickly. As adults we use metaphors to help us clarify ideas. Metaphors are used to enhance explanations by calling upon words which apply similar concepts, even though they don't belong to the same class. For instance, we "shoot down" an idea. No one takes a gun to an idea, but the words used in that instance underscore the rejection of the idea. Children use metaphor in their pretend play. For instance, any object can signify another even though to an adult there is no relationship to the other (a curved stick can be a telephone to the child). Engaging in these pretend situations expands the child's thinking, creates better word usage, and develops his mental abilities to understand language.

Parents can foster pretend or fantasy play by:

- encouraging the activity;
- creating places for the child to play;
- not interfering or imposing "rules";
- becoming active and willing participants in the play when appropriate.

The more youngsters engage in this kind of activity, the more they explore what is and is not possible. It draws the child's play toward something that is more real. Eventually, of course, the child needs to have experiences that appear real and work in real life. That's the key to better development. The youngster must test how one person reacts to the other, reinforcing her own and the other's positions in a society. This can be done very harmlessly in play but not so harmlessly in real life.

Games played with the child, even the infant, are meaningful. Let him make sense of his world. Don't clutter his life with contrived toys or situations for play. The simpler, the better. Encourage play, make space for it, and keep it on the child's level so that he can use it for his needs.

Use play for verbalization, naming, new words, categorizing objects, and pretending. Give the child the opportunity to explore, but be sensitive to potentially harmful or dangerous situations that might occur within her play space.

Up to two years of age, the child's world is right there in the family. After that, social interaction with other children will increase dramatically.

Pretend play, which becomes a strong part of the toddler's life with dolls and toys of all sorts, is different from the social play that follows. The social play, which involves others, is characterized by give and take. Although pretend play can be in fits and starts with lots of changes in interest and direction during short periods of time, it lays the foundation for important imaginative and social play that will last for years.

When children in a family are close in age, or when, as is the case today, toddlers are in day-care situations, pretend play moves the child more quickly toward social play.

Make-believe should be encouraged in children, because it encourages the use of imagination. Children become adventuresome, less fearful about new situations, and they also become more willing to act creatively.

I've noted that, in many families, as the children initiate creative or adventuresome play, parents begin to meddle in it.

That's not a good idea. Kids should learn to experiment on their own and learn what works and what doesn't work in various situations, alone, and with other children. This independence builds confidence, security, and also an interest in play activities.

Social play begins in early childhood, and, although some people think that it stops by the beginning school years, I believe it extends in many instances through adult life.

The advantages and uses of social play are largely related to language development, that is, learning how to communicate— not only with others but with the world. The more social play the child experiences, the more opportunity he has to verbalize situations and formulate real-life models. If play has no reality attached to it, kids will become uninterested and abandon it. If kids are going to solve problems through play, the play must be real.

The older the child gets, the greater the chance that ideas of expected behavior or rules are imposed from outside. At this point kids learn that in social situations you must respect others and act accordingly. This is appropriate since it sets the stage for the behavior that allows people within a society to respect one another and not take advantage of each other. Thus, play becomes a bridge to adulthood. Kids learn that under some circumstances you act one way and under others you act differently. Kids are noisy in playgrounds and quieter in school.

As we impose rules on our lives, play becomes games. As I've said, games have imposed rules and there is a clear idea that the purpose of the game is to win or lose. We've talked about games in a previous chapter so I'll only restate that games:

- should be enjoyable, without undue pressure to win.
- should be for the child's sake, not the parents';
- should teach the child to be fair and honest;
- should encourage discipline and hard work;
- should be kept in proper perspective (that means there are other things in life).

The importance of play as a vehicle for development in the child cannot be overstated. It must be appreciated that the content of play, increasingly imposed by adults, can also have a strong negative impact on the child. Activities and toys of violence, for example, have become commonplace as entertainment for children. Parents should realize that play is a training ground for their children and should not be regarded lightly. It must be used for positive, not negative, learning.

Let's get back to play as an adult behavior, because I think it has a real place in our lives.

Some time ago one of my classmates, who happened to play baseball, told me he often dreamed of standing at home plate in Yankee Stadium and hitting a baseball out of the park. This sort of daydream or pretend play has a continuing place in our lives since our dreams and expectations keep life going for us. I think it keeps us looking up, not down, and helps us take on new challenges. This is an extension of the childhood play phenomenon of which I've been speaking.

Play leads to imagination, fantasy, creativity, and a whole host of advantages that help shape our lives as children and adults. Without play, none of the creativity important to the development of the child's capabilities will emerge.

7

Understanding

Take time to think—it's the source of power.

The essential part of communication is understanding. Without understanding you cannot exchange ideas, and the exchange of ideas is what communication is all about. Understanding is developed in the child through a series of steps that begin in infancy and continue into adult life. These steps begin with the naming of objects and people during infancy. The child begins to acquire many new concepts during the early years of life that give understanding to his world. For a period of time the child's concepts about things around him are greater than the language she has to describe them. In time, the child will identify abstract ideas which allow her to comprehend even the most difficult presentations.

Two things are vital for developing good communication skills in children. First, the skills must be developed in sequence, each dependent upon the other. As is the case with many abilities in children, one forms the base for the next. Second, the *interaction* between adult and child must involve a response from the child. The interaction between the teacher and the student, or between you and your child, must demand that the child respond appropriately. This keeps the child from being a passive participant in the process. When a child is passive you have no indication of his understanding, nor do you have the opportunity to build on the conversation.

Emerging communication skills must be used regularly or they won't develop properly. It's not enough for you to act like a TV set. That is passive communication. We know from studies of little children that passive teaching soon becomes background noise to which they do not respond. You need to listen, question, and respond so that the youngster is thinking while learning, so that she is taking an active part in the conversation. Everything you do with your child while she's learning must stretch her ability.

The cardinal elements of the development of comprehension in the child are:

- a solid base of names and concepts;
- good language ability;
- ongoing experience;
- regular information exchange;
- broad exposure;
- problem-solving opportunities;
- verbalization;
- a growing vocabulary.

When you link understanding to language development, you're on the right track. The better your child is able to use language, the better he'll understand those around him.

Language, on one level, is used to identify things and to express wishes and needs. This is how the infant uses it. Building upon this level the toddler or preschooler eventually uses words to express ideas that will establish a working relationship with his world, through parents, friends, and playmates. In time, as the child's language skills mature, he uses language in a much more abstract way. This allows him to question and to understand the workings of the world. It is from this abstract level that the growing child brings his own abilities to bear on the world in order to contribute to it rather than just to take from it. These steps take perhaps eight or ten years to evolve, but it is important to realize that without the ongoing input of the parent real understanding will never occur.

In our efforts to help the child pass from the primary stages of communication to more advanced levels we're attempting to bring the child's inborn abilities to the surface.

It has long been my belief that child development is completely based on language development. You can't have one without the other. All of the skills or functions that I discuss in this book revolve around language or communication skills. Some things are obvious and some not so obvious. Certainly the child's intellectual or academic skills are directly related to language. We've shown in previous chapters that social skills help form language ability, and motor skills contribute to the overall development of the youngster. These are all under the direct control of language. I propose that emotional development is equally as important as social development in the maturation of the child's abilities, and that it is directly related to language.

The understanding that forms the base for good communication during life has its foundation in the maturation of language skills which begins during infancy.

The first step in developing language is to get the words and the names of things in place, including basic colors, shapes, and sizes. You start at home, in the park, or at the store. That's where you can teach children colors or sizes or shapes. After these are in place, get started on the basic concepts.

The second step is mastering concepts like *in front of* or *behind, up and down, over and under,* as well as categories, like fruits or vegetables or dairy products. These are natural, everyday concepts encountered in the home or at the grocery store. They allow the child to build one concept upon the other.

On the market today are books, games, and other helpers that attract the attention of children and stress word meanings or concepts.

A familiar environment is the best place to introduce these early learning steps to the child. It also reinforces the training for the parent because it creates a habit of using every opportunity to teach her child.

Parents must realize that children need this base of information in place prior to entering kindergarten if they are to get the most out of that learning experience.

In teaching words and concepts, there are simple steps to be taken:

- Use the term.
- Show what it means.
- Ask what it means.
- Use examples.

The basic skills must become automatic, which means that they are learned so well they are used without ever thinking about them.

Understanding is the goal to be achieved through the exchange of information. In your conversations with the child use a word or concept in several different ways. Always use reinforcement to solidify the learning experience. You can try the newspaper reporter game, for example, in which the child relates daily events using the concepts or words learned.

If you enjoy the interaction with your youngster he'll take your lead. There is no substitute for a good role model. He'll come to value learning, which is an important lesson to learn from a parent.

I recently came across the following ten commandments for parents of gifted children. However, these rules really apply to all parents and to all children.

Parents' Ten Commandments for Gifted Children

1. Parents must serve as role models to the child.
2. Foster security and independence through praise and demonstrated love.
3. Interaction with your child must be a life-style.
4. Encourage your child in all aspects of life, keeping fantasy alive while disciplining the imagination.
5. Enrich your child, particularly through active inquiry.
6. Develop critical thought through questions, shared experiences, and elicited responses.
7. Achieve the delicate balance between freedom and control.
8. Keep the child focused so that productivity does not suffer because of creativity.
9. Insist upon speculation as a constant associate.
10. Achieve discipline, both intellectual as well as physical, for without it no gift becomes reality.

It is critical that parents get involved with their children if the children are to develop their potential fully. It should be the aim of all parents to create a life-style of involvement and interaction with their children. In that way only will parents help their youngsters become successful adults.

Keep the language that you use with your child crisp, clear, and simple. Also keep it correct. As you interact with your own youngster, help her use words correctly and in the right place.

Don't be negative with the child. Keep it positive. For instance, as a step in language development, children will use the common suffix -ed on the end of the present tense to create the past tense even when it's not appropriate. Thus *go* becomes *goed*. In time, the child will adapt to irregular conjugations, like *went*, and use them properly. If the youngster keeps up the use of *goed* when he should be saying *went,* it's appropriate to urge him to use the correct form. Do this by saying, "That's right, he went." Do this a few times—if it doesn't seem to be taking, gradually say to the child, "Say 'He went' instead of 'He goed.'"

Clean up the child's language during these early school years. Insist upon or urge correct pronunciation of words. Again, don't be negative, don't criticize. Just offer the correct way of doing it.

I also think it's fair to clean up the child's language by eliminating foul or socially unacceptable language from her vocabulary. I know they all hear it on the school bus or on the playground, but learning not to use it has to begin somewhere. That somewhere is usually at home. Establish a pattern of acceptable speech at home, at dinner, or around you. It goes without saying that this means you must clean up your own speech. If kids hear four-letter words out of Mom's mouth, it's obviously acceptable to use them. Don't let your child learn that.

Get your child to be careful about language so explanations are just that, explanations that really clarify what the child is trying to express. Insist upon reasonably clear speech that gets the story out without wasting time or straying from the point. Kids do ramble on sometimes. Don't discourage their storytelling by interrupting them with corrections in their speech. Be tolerant and helpful, but use the opportunity to teach good language usage.

Many children use simple or restricted speech without introducing an elaboration of ideas. This limits the message they can convey and limits their use of language. Other children expand upon ideas, elaborating stories and building upon concepts.

If the child does not get used to a more elaborated speech then she will never develop the familiarity with language or the vocabulary necessary to express ideas clearly. When she needs particular words to explain a particular idea, neither the words nor the way of using them will be available to the child. Just as the brain needs constant work to remain sharp and active so does the child's speech.

Children develop the speech patterns and usage that are available in their environment. Parents must work at good speech if they expect it of their children.

The first big stumbling block to understanding that many children experience in school is often math-related.

Math is a language. It is composed of symbols, meanings, concepts, and rules, just like any other language. There are basic elements to be learned and to be made automatic, just as there are with the words and grammar of English.

In math we first learn the sequence of numbers. We call them one, two, three, and so forth by agreement. Next we learn the concepts, like addition, subtraction, and so forth, and the rules that allow us to manipulate numbers. We need to understand these rules so we can explain why $3 - 2 = 1$. After the basics are in place we need to have exposure to a series of increasingly difficult concepts that give us flexibility in the use of this mathematical language. Eventually we get to the point where we are familiar with all of the ways in which the language can be used to our advantage. Some parts of the system, like any language, should be committed to memory and made automatic. In days gone by we all learned to add automatically. Today calculators have taken over that function so adding quickly may soon become a lost art. We also used to learn our multiplication tables by heart. This was a ritual of the grammar school math class.

I still believe that committing the multiplication tables to memory ought to be one of the mental disciplines for the grammar-school child. It's good mental training, and, also, who knows, someday your calculator might be without power.

I stress understanding in math because it becomes a critical part of doing science in the middle and upper school years. The advantage of science to a child lies not so much in the understanding of our world and how it works but in the opportunity for problem solving. Children need to learn how to think a problem through to a solution. One of the beauties of science is the order that occurs. This is very helpful to the young mind trying to understand nature.

It's a good idea to have your child explain things about which he is speaking. This is particularly true for math. Don't hesitate to ask why something happens or why a math answer is true. Get him used to understanding concepts and being able to express them.

Some school math programs focus on concepts using Cuisenaire rods and other learning tools to make the ideas more concrete. Often children use terms like base numbers correctly, but fail to apply the concept to other areas. Parents can help by discussing homework assignments to reinforce comprehension. Similar interest and discussion will strengthen ideas for their children in all subject areas.

Early in the school experience teachers ask children to do reports on different places, like Mexico or Canada. Usually the report follows some preparation of reading or discussion that has been part of the regular school program. In the report, the child usually presents information about the country: where it is on the map, what the climate is like, what the people are like, and what they do, from work to customs. Through these efforts the child develops an understanding of the country and its heritage.

This underscores that we can't learn a word or a concept through simply defining it or naming it. You have to use the word and understand how it applies in a particular situation. When we come across the word *Mexico* we gradually develop an understanding of the culture and of the people which gives the true meaning behind the name of the country. Eventually we find that there are many meanings to some words and there are many facets to the word.

The child's comprehension of his world is assembled through an understanding of people, cultures, and geographical locations.

Understanding emerges with knowledge, with familiarity. Language is the key to that knowledge and opens the door to understanding. The better we represent an idea, the easier it is to learn, conceptualize, and remember.

We as adults have some of the same problems that are seen in children. Children look at information from the only perspective that is available to them. Their learning is slanted in the direction in which it is presented. Some of the "facts" that we know or talk about are true, but much is open to further information. We need to take this into consideration as we attempt to provide answers for the questioning child. Sometimes it's not so easy to give both sides of the picture.

The psychologist Jean Piaget suggested that children develop their intellect by acquiring information through new experiences. Each time this occurs the new information readjusts the old information. Sooner or later, within the limitations of the child's ability and within the limitations of what is known, the child's experiences lead him to what is accepted as reality. Since we don't know everything there is to know, there's always something new on the horizon to be learned. The child needs to keep gathering new information. As he sifts through the new data, comparing it to the old, he arrives at a better understanding of all things.

This brings me to the point of adding into the child's learning, along with the three R's, some ongoing introduction to some of the events that are taking place in the world around her. By the late grammar-school years children should have enough background information to tune into both state and federal elections, conflicts in various locations around the globe, issues of the environment, hunger, education, and more. These subjects are talked about on TV news or written about in the newspaper and are often represented in conversation at home or in school. Get children to examine the elements that go into any one of these issues to allow better understanding. This process guides the child's thinking toward a concern for others and away from the more self-centered thinking of the younger child. This step is critical to abstract thought and makes the child comprehend the interaction among people at home and in the world. The best vehicle for this is the TV set. Programs that meet the needs of the child by developing information about an array of topics are available. They all require parental interaction.

As soon as is practical, substitute the child's version of *National Geographic* or similar publications for children. Then move on to the weekly news magazines.

This experience is important to the child's development of adult understanding, and it provides a fund of information upon which the child can build for upper school years and adult life. Parents must understand that the child's progression from the early mastery of basic information to the comprehension of abstract thought demands regular application of experience and learning. The end result of sophisticated understanding will not occur without careful attention to learning during the early years.

Children's minds need to unfold like flowers, and that doesn't happen without a constant flow of information, interaction, questions, answers, thinking, and problem solving.

Our complaints about what our kids know or how much is demanded of them in school are often misplaced. Many youngsters go off to school unprepared, without the skills to accept the program that they meet there. Teachers assume that basic skills are in place when the child arrives at school. It's true that the schools often fail to encourage learning through discipline and work. It is also true that many kids don't do enough to learn today what is necessary for tomorrow. By the time someone asks what they understand, the opportunity is lost, and it was lost on the home front.

The responsibility of the home is to provide:

- good examples;
- basic information;
- basic skills;
- constant reading exposure;
- discussion between parent and child;

- frequent praise and approval;
- discipline;
- good language use;
- regular learning excursions;
- interest and understanding.

If the above responsibility of the home has been set in motion and is kept in motion the school becomes a willing accomplice to the whole business of child development. Understanding falls into place in a very natural way.

8

Experience and Enrichment

Take time to look around—the day is too short to be selfish.

Parents must regularly provide experiences for their children during their developmental years. An introduction to life events is the basis for learning. Through such exposure children gain a familiarity with their world that lets potential turn into ability. Some life experiences are less common than others and go beyond those ordinarily offered in school or at home. They extend the dimensions of experience to allow the child to see parallels between past and present. They offer the opportunity to understand people, values, and motivation that are common among societies across the ages. We call these experiences enrichment. Through enrichment some have brought perfection to ordinary happenings.

Let me separate experience and enrichment and explain the obligations and advantages associated with each.

Experience

The experience of the child begins in the nursery. His tools are his senses, but the force behind the ongoing lessons is you, the parent.

Be mindful of the fact that children must be prepared to learn. They must eventually take to the classroom a body of knowledge that includes the names of things; concepts that allow an understanding of everything, from shapes and sizes to position in space; and skills for listening and learning. This primary information provides the base upon which the child's ordinary growth and everyday existence rely. Survival in a complex society requires reading and writing, productive and functional skills, and an understanding of the forces that regulate life in that society.

Learning and the path to full development are constructed in layers. Early experiences provide basic skills that open opportunities for more learning. Your child's exposure to new experiences must happen in a progression, and there is a time for each step.

Time has become a precious commodity to today's parent, so a regular and planned involvement with your child is mandatory if you are to provide him with experiences.

Trips, excursions, walks, and just keeping company with your child are a pleasure for you both and a terrific way to broaden the child's experience. There's something to be learned in all sorts of situations. Kids can refine visual identification skills by collecting different tree leaves and taking them home to match each leaf with a particular tree pictured in a book. On the other hand, a trip might be to a local museum that tells you about your town 100 or 150 years ago. If you investigate you'll find many opportunities available to you at your doorstep. The first step in the development of a habit of shared experiences with your child is to identify what's available in your immediate community, and then start using it.

I think of the categories of experiences as:

- General
- Entertainment
- Cultural
- Historical
- Scientific

Each category has its place in the life of the child. Also, every child should be exposed to all of them. Don't make an expert of your child too soon. Some children know everything about cars, but they have never heard of Abraham Lincoln.

Think of the many places created for children in most towns and cities. There are wonderful children's museums in many communities that have different themes at different times of the year, and that actively encourage participation of the child in the experience. Science museums have made spaceships for children and have developed technology for involving even the most sophisticated child. Learning experiences can involve children in everything from planting trees to watching performing arts. Children all need pieces of this important pie.

There are many businesses that proudly explain to children (and parents) how shoes are made or how their favorite ice cream is created. Plymouth Plantation, here in southeastern Massachusetts, is staffed by guides who speak only seventeenth-century English to complete the flavor and the learning experience.

There is one thing that these opportunities cannot do, and that is get your child to them. That's your job. And the quality of the experience for the child is dependent upon your enthusiasm, your preparation for the excursion, and your interaction with your child. Do not put it off. Start now.

In our society the experiences I've discussed will usually be considered ordinary, but what of those that are outside the ordinary?

Enrichment

There is great emphasis on the parents' responsibility to entertain their children during their sometimes limited time together. Disney World, an amusement park, or the beach are favorite entertainments. They are enjoyable and they have their place. But what about that Saturday or Sunday afternoon when the parent can blend pleasure and learning into one activity?

Enrichment activities, which I will designate as art, music, drama, dance, literature, poetry, history, and even science, broaden the horizons of the child by introducing her to information and ideas about people and places of today and yesterday, adding a dimension of learning that is beyond the ordinary. Enrichment activities foster a curiosity and involvement in learning. They also give the child some insight into the thought, the values, and the achievements of people throughout history.

To achieve successful introduction into this world of enrichment, the parent must be as interested and excited as he intends the child to be. Share your enthusiasm and create a natural exchange.

It's hard to change the habits of a teenager who is used to amusement parks. Begin exposure to cultural events at an early age to create an interest in enriching activities. Don't lose the child to a lifetime of only being entertained. Get the child involved. Learning must be balanced with recreation or the child will resent the intrusion on his free time. An unwilling participant in some cultural event is hardly likely to learn anything or find the experience pleasurable.

It is not unusual for children to experience a delayed appreciation of the activity to which they are exposed. Many watch their first ballet at four years of age and grow to enjoy the experience as an adult.

Enrichment has its place in and outside the home. Through reading stories together (or telling stories), watching videos, listening to music, and discussing each, parents can create a wonderful exposure to the arts at home. Outside the home, attending ballets, going to the theater, visiting museums, and experiencing historic sites provide invaluable enrichment. The key to all of this activity is *informed interaction*.

Before attending any play or ballet, introduce your child to the story. If you and your child are familiar with the characters and the action of the plot, you'll enjoy the performance more and have time to observe the sets, music, and costumes and to get some meaning from each.

The perfect first ballet is *The Nutcracker* at Christmastime. No child can resist the wonder and fantasy of Clara's dream. However, your enthusiasm as the parent must be real if your child is to be receptive.

There is a real advantage for the child if the play or ballet has a child in a major role, as is the case with the musical *Oliver*. The identification by the child with the story is easier. It's enriching for your child to listen to a story about a difficult life for a child in another setting.

Preparation for a visit to a museum or historic landmark is a must. Follow-up activities can include bread baking at home or candle making to appreciate differences between then and now. Try to tie people and events of former days to today. This will strengthen the child's understanding.

Anytime a trip, near or far, is planned, do some serious preparation. Do some reading yourself so that your discussion is informative and directed toward your child's interests. List the must-see places and why. Get your child involved. Let him do some research to get basic facts and historical background.

If there's a special exhibit at some museum, plan to visit. Remember, there's a reason why children think of museums as dreary and dreadful places. They often don't know what they're looking at or why. That is the result of a lack of preparation. Get them to view the museum as a place to satisfy curiosity, spark an interest, and learn something new. The experience has to be interesting and worthwhile right then, not when the child grows up. Children don't want to hear, "You'll thank me when you're older." Also, focus the visit. Find out what you want to see and stick to those places. Some museums have too much to take in on a single visit. Make your trip leisurely, enjoyable, and informative, but not so informative that it's boring.

Watch for special science shows that offer hands-on approaches to learning. Audience participation goes a long way with kids. Think of activities that can be done at home to reinforce concepts presented at the show.

Go stargazing with your child. Learn about the constellations and see how many you can identify. A visit to the nearest planetarium is a terrific outing for your child. Again, be prepared to answer questions with authority.

At home, introduce enrichment activities at bedtime. Children love to have stories read to them. Introduce a wide variety of themes early so your child develops an interest in history, mythology, science, the arts, and other areas from which you can draw. There are fables, myths, and folktales that fascinate children and enrich our daily lives and language.

One of the time-honored ways of getting children to enjoy history is to read historical novels, or tell stories about historical characters who can be made real and approachable. Try someone colorful like Henry VIII or his daughter, Queen Elizabeth, as a good starting place for interesting people.

Classic stories, like Robin Hood, *A Thousand and One Nights, The Wind in the Willows,* and *Anne of Green Gables,* are perfect bedtime reading, one chapter at a time.

Even the television or VCR can be a source of family enrichment. Establish a compromise between entertainment and educational television. There are many movies of the past, aimed at children, that are presented on public broadcasting stations. Often children would rather watch than read, so the TV can be used to advantage here. Movies and videotapes are an important medium for teaching if we exercise standards.

Don't forget music. Radio, TV, and tapes, records, or CDs can be used to introduce your child to all kinds of music. If your child has no exposure to classical music or jazz or folk music, he'll never develop this side of his learning and he will miss an important piece of life.

Our children grew up in the era of the late Arthur Fiedler, who conducted the Boston Pops and contributed much to music appreciation by all. On each Fourth of July the Pops would give an evening outdoor concert along the banks of the Charles River, and thousands would congregate to hear it. The finale, always punctuated by fireworks, was spectacular. Although the music was light, it helped to build a love for good music that is lasting. In many communities children's concerts and music appreciation presentations are available to encourage their interest.

No matter what the event, children should be prepared for the experience. During the days preceding the performance introduce the child to the work, its story, what's to be seen or heard, and some background information to the best of your ability. Preparation pays off because it allows maximum appreciation of the presentation. Remember that the better you prepare a child for such a performance, the greater the likelihood is he'll come back for more.

Why bother with enrichment? Why not let those who are so inclined seek out their interest and let the others march to the beat of the drum that they hear?

We know from child-development studies that children must be exposed to things to set learning in motion. We also know that children must develop, beyond their base of information, experiences which will provide the background for understanding, problem solving, and abstract thought. This expansion is what enrichment is all about.

What about the parent who has no background from which to initiate these learning experiences? Learn together. Use the excursions and the enrichment to help yourself as well as your child. Take the time to learn. Don't run and hide. You are not alone. There are opportunities for parents as well as for children.

My strongest advice to parents is to introduce experiences and enrichment to your children early and keep the interest alive through your own active involvement. Keep a perspective, but never abandon the job. Your willingness to continue to develop and participate in your child's interests will bear fruit.

Encourage self-sufficiency and independence. Take the time to keep up with your child's interests and needs so that your ongoing interaction is meaningful and productive. Get your child to believe in herself and in her abilities. As she expands her learning, her capability will grow, and with it her confidence and the development of her potential.

9

Reading

Take time to read—it's the foundation of wisdom.

Of all the skills that a child must master, reading is probably the most useful and also the most lasting. It offers us entrance into a world of learning and wonderment and, in time, gives us a continuing interface with our world as well as companionship.

Reading is one of those activities that must be accomplished in two stages: first, you have to learn how to do it and, second, you have to understand what you're reading. Even though you can pronounce the words perfectly, until you understand what you're reading you are not communicating. Communication is the heart of reading.

Reading is a skill that demands practice. Unless you keep at it on a regular basis, you'll lose the ability. Doing it regularly not only improves the quality of reading but it also increases the reader's familiarity with his language. This is a critical step in understanding what he reads.

To comprehend ideas and thoughts easily you have to use language all the time. Reading is a developed habit, not a lesson that you learn in school. It is ideally taught in the home. So that's what I'm going to talk about in this chapter: how you the parent can make your child into a reader.

What does it take to read?

How do we go about teaching this skill which seems to occupy so much effort and attention of parents, teachers, and a host of other professionals? In fact, there seems to be a certain amount of mystery that surrounds the ability to read. There are literally dozens of ways that have been devised to teach children how to master reading, and, seemingly, no matter what we do, most learn almost in spite of the method used.

Despite this, everyone seems to be searching for a better way to get children to read. Even high-school teachers want to discover some magic that will encourage their students to pick up a book. First they want to teach them to read, then they want to *get* them to read.

All children begin to read by going through the same steps, some more quickly than others, to be sure, but nevertheless all must master the same steps. These physical, or more properly, psychological skills are very simple, although they are difficult for some children.

There are four steps children must take in order to read:

1. They must learn shapes, like circles, squares, and triangles. Shapes make up the letters of our alphabet.

2. They must learn the alphabet. Many parents teach their children the alphabet using picture books or other tools starting at about two years of age. Some children are five or six years old before it's all in place.

3. They must begin to associate sounds with the letters of the alphabet. This is done by playing games or singing songs that get the letters to say their sounds.

4. They must blend or join the individual sounds of the letters into groups that become words. Blending is easy for some and a real trial for others.

Once the child has mastered these four steps, she is ready to read.

Over the years in our schools, we have gone back and forth, using one form of reading instruction or another. Each was either a "sight" method or one that stressed "sound." Although we still find some areas using the "look/say" approach, it has been shown that children do better with some form of phonics that demands that words be "sounded out" as they are read. In truth, youngsters learn to read with their ears, not with their eyes. It's obvious that we need to look at the printed word, but what we "read" is what makes sense to us. This is an important concept for a parent to understand because it clarifies what has to be done to make a reader of your child.

I'll give you some examples of this.

If I write "John hit the ball with a *brat*," you'll read *bat* for *brat* since the word *brat* doesn't make any sense to us in that sentence. Your brain ignores the *r* in the word. As many of you know, it can be very difficult to pick up errors in the morning newspaper unless you are trained to proofread.

A child with dyslexia, who has trouble learning to read, often continues to read like the beginning reader. His brain miscalls what he reads and it doesn't make sense until he learns his language well enough to understand what belongs or doesn't belong. In order to teach this child to read effectively you have to stress what makes sense, not spend hours and hours worrying about the errors he makes as he struggles with the printed word. I think this is why we have had so much difficulty teaching children with dyslexia during the past twenty-five years. The emphasis was in the wrong place.

Good readers aren't born—they are made at home.

It is true, however, that some do it earlier. One day I sat at breakfast in the kitchen of a fellow physician and the nearly four-year-old child in the family crawled up onto my lap and asked me if I would like to hear her reading. I think that I was more interested in my first cup of coffee, so I paid little attention to the child until suddenly I became aware that she was actually reading the book in her hands. This got my attention quickly, so I flipped to another page or two to see if she had memorized a passage on the page in front of me. Like clockwork, she moved through each page without much hesitation. She carefully pronounced each word and strung them together as the author intended. Amazing! I asked the child's mother, who obviously was used to the whole performance, how long the girl had been reading (after all, children do not usually read before they are four). The answer was, "About six months." That was even more unusual—reading at three and a half!

Let's look at how parents can develop reading skills in their children.

1. The first step is to set an example and create experience with reading. Parents cannot begin reading to their children too early. I know that some have said to me that they feel silly reading a story to an infant. Never mind, it's the beginning of a habit for the parent as well as for the child. You talk to your infant and he doesn't understand what you say. Early reading to an infant has been shown to exert a calming effect, to strengthen the parent/child bond, and to lead the infant to associate the voice of the parent with a secure environment. This sets the stage for reading as an interactive process between parent and child.

2. The second step is to bathe your youngster in language. Talk to him, read to him, and make it a habit to share experiences wherever you go or wherever you are.

3. Next in line is working on the base of information such as the shapes and names and sounds of the letters of the alphabet. This demands that the child become more familiar with the forms and shapes in her environment. Get her to experience her world.

4. Now we use the books and information available to us to get the child into the habit of reading. This gets reinforced at home, at school, and through trips to the local library and

the like. This is a critical stage, for if you hand the job over
to school and simply reinforce what the school expects of
the child, interest will wane. Schools cannot keep a child
tuned into reading; that has to come from the home.
Research has demonstrated that unless books are available
and the home reinforces reading, early ability in reading
will diminish.

5. The next phase is the use of reading by the child. This
   involves everything from schoolwork to entertainment. The
   parent must keep the flame alive by encouraging reading as
   a source of information as well as a source of enjoyment.
   Otherwise the TV/video world will overcome the child very
   quickly. Remember, the whole idea of children's program-
   ming on TV has very little to do with what's best for the
   child and a great deal to do with what's best for the
   advertisers and the cash flow. Don't let your child down.
   He needs you to establish some worthwhile habits that will
   persist in his life.

6. Finally, you should impose on the child the whole idea of
   learning something in depth. This takes reading. You
   cannot become well informed about anything unless you're
   willing to take the time to seek out as much information as
   is available. Quality is no longer required of many in our
   society so they are content to get an idea from a magazine
   article or a TV program and let it go at that. It's your job as
   the parent to create the environment that makes quality
   standard in your home.

These six steps focus on the home, take some time, and must
be set in motion before bad habits take hold. This means that you
start early and keep at it. I appreciate that it's a lot easier to put
your feet up after a long hard day rather than make part of your
home routine the training that leads to good reading habits.
Think of it in another way: this is not something that you'd like
to do but something that you must do. If you do it right, it's a lot
easier than you think.

Attitude is a critical factor in making your home one that

encourages good reading skills in a child. Begin by collecting books, especially those books that you may have listened to or read as a child yourself. This way the child will not only sense your own enthusiasm for the books but in time, when she is old enough to understand that this was one of your favorites as a child, it will take on special meaning to her. Create a home library of children's books that can be constantly available to the child and that demonstrates your interest in books.

Ask for books for your child as gifts. Interrupt the constant flow of stuffed animals from doting grandparents—get some books. What if someone says he never knows which ones to buy? Let him to do some exploring at the library or at the bookstore. Ask the local librarian, who will usually be an excellent resource. Keep a list yourself. Comb through bookstores. Watch for books that have won children's book awards—they are often gems.

My aunt was a browser. She knew of several bookstores in Boston and Cambridge where she was able to sit for hours reading parts of stories or simply thumbing through books to judge their quality or their desirability. She usually knew the books worth reading. She browsed during her lunchtime, or after work, or on a Saturday morning. Sometimes she took me browsing, which is a good habit to acquire.

There are four kinds of children's books for preschoolers:

1. Picture books that let children recognize a letter or an animal and keep the story, if there is one, to a minimum.

2. Stories that are meant to be read to children. These are my favorites, since the author has gone to some length to create a special tale for the child.

3. Stories that may be a little too long or complex for the young child at his age, so they take some editing or additional storytelling on the part of the reader.

4. Books that are truly meant for the beginning reader.

How do you find these without making a career out of browsing in bookstores? Your best resources are the local librarian in charge of children's books and the person at your bookstore who's familiar with children's books. Beyond these, you can ask friends about the books that their children read, and you can consult some of the lists published by the American Library Association, by the Library of Congress, or in the numerous books about children's reading.

Keep your audience in mind. Keep the child's developmental needs and abilities in mind, also. Infants like sounds, bright colors, and textures. They also like to chew on the pages. Toddlers want visual experiences and stories repeated over and over again, thus the popularity and durability of Mother Goose stories and Dr. Seuss. The older the child gets, the more content—from factual information, to experiences with which the child can relate, to suspense—must be provided in the book.

One of the great advantages of reading to your child is your appreciation of his interest and his understanding. By the time some child enter elementary school their reading tastes have progressed well beyond their peers'. Don't kill their enjoyment of reading by boring them to death.

There should be rules for reading in every home:

1. Never stop reading to your children, even when they are good readers. This is a valuable source of communication throughout the school years—make it part of every day.

2. Make sure that you are familiar with the books that your children read.

3. Boring books should be discarded.

4. Teach children to learn from books, noting or underlining important parts.

5. Create time for reading that is pleasurable and doesn't conflict with other responsibilities.

6. Save the good books, commenting on the enjoyment and value they'll provide for the next reader—or generation!

Become familiar with the person in charge of the children's section of the library. Ask what's available: books, programs, read-aloud sessions, and interesting presentations for your child's participation. Get your child comfortable with the library as a friendly place to visit and learn.

Establish in your child the habit of going to the library. Make it part of his life so he looks forward to his excursions with enthusiasm. Many libraries have children's sessions on a regular basis for reading and discussion, or for the presentation of a particular theme or topic. These are good learning sessions and they develop good habits in children. Encourage your child to take books home for reading and let her select those books that she intends to read. Influence the quality of the selection, but don't kill the child's enthusiasm for participating in the decision making.

Libraries were always formidable in the past. Everything was quiet and orderly. No talking allowed. That's changing for the better. There needs to be a glass wall between the children's section and the rest of the library where people need quiet. Children should ask questions—that's how they learn. They are normally noisy. Know what your child enjoys in his reading and in his listening. Give him some variety—it goes a long way. Adventure stories may be interesting to you but your child may like some mystery or fantasy. Mix it up. Eventually your child will appreciate a wide variety in his reading.

Let your child set the pace of reading and storytelling during your reading times with her. If she wants to stop and ask questions, take the opportunity to talk and discuss the ideas that are in the story. If a story seems uninteresting to the child, bail out. Move on to another story. Sense if your child has had too much for the moment, or is too tired for a session at that time.

In our household we often used bedtime as story reading or storytelling time. Sometimes the child just wants to talk. I like to encourage the art of storytelling because it adds a personal touch that many children like. Try it, you'll like it! You don't have to be a movie star to tell your child a story. After all, your youngster wants to hear his mom or dad. You're the one he looks up to.

One more thing about reading with your child: the story may

be too long for the child, or you may find that it's too tiring all in one setting. Set some natural break, leaving the child with something to look forward to the next evening. When you return to the story the next evening, let the child fill you in. What's the tale about? That's a good way to help with understanding and memory.

Use stories as a take-off point for an excursion. If your child liked Robert McCloskey's *Blueberries for Sale,* then you might organize an outing to a farm where your child can experience blueberry picking (something that's very easy on Cape Cod but not so easy in New York). There the child could do some picking for himself, and the berries might end up in a blueberry pie.

A story in a book should become a journey or an interesting event, not just something between two covers on a book. Keep storytelling alive, get into the story yourself so that both of you enjoy it. Create a fascinating world for your child. Use stories as an opportunity to enrich your child about your own likes as a child or experiences that were favorites of yours. Children like to share these experiences with a parent and make them come alive.

Take your child to children's plays, puppet theaters, movies, and the like for through these he will become increasingly familiar with stories that came from books that you might have already read or will read in the future. Think of the magic of Walt Disney enjoyed by millions of children. His tales are presented on videos, in books, in the movies, and at the Disney amusement parks. Talk to your child about these stories, what was different, or interesting, or unexpected. Perhaps some part of the story was confusing to your youngster. Talk about it. You'll learn about your child and things that are important to him that you might have been unaware of. Give your child the experience of listening and reading. Avoid the habit of many to confine learning to visual events. Reading and language are also auditory skills and need reinforcement.

By the time your child is in school and reading, the approach to reading encouragement takes a slightly different path. Now the child's attention span is longer, her interests have become more mature. Learning matters to the child particularly during these early years. The competition at school and at home for attention, approval, and results heightens. Kids like to please at this time in their lives and you need to keep up your efforts to involve yourself in their learning. This is the time when many parents seem to leave it to others. Keep your influence high. Never give up on the reading at home.

I want to emphasize the importance of reading and continuing to read to a child well into elementary school and beyond. We did this in our own home until the kids were so busy with their schoolwork that we couldn't find the time to do so. Many parents feel that once their child learns to read the child should do all of the reading. This is not true. The importance of reading is discussion and exchange of ideas that come out of the story. Children also need to hear adults read to refine their own reading style, to pay attention to punctuation, and to learn to put some emphasis where it belongs. Reading should be learned as a pleasurable experience for people of all ages.

It's good practice in reading to allow children to anticipate a story or an ending. Let them tell you what's going to happen on the next page or at the end of the story. This causes them to think the story through and to use the information that they've acquired. It is good training for the days to come in school and in adult life.

As children get older it's a good habit to use much longer books for the source of reading material. Let the children follow the tale with interest and expectation. Give your child the opportunity to think.

Reading must become a life-style that supports all aspects of the child's learning, and supports his continued interest in learning.

Traditionally, school has been presented as an unpleasant ritual that all children experience. In fact, school should be described as an opportunity. It is the child's only opportunity to prepare for life. It is not just something that a child does during the day, but it is his job. It is the full-time activity of children from five or six years of age to at least eighteen. For some it's enjoyable hard work and for others it's a deadly burden, mostly because they have trouble doing the job. The biggest problem experienced that causes school to be difficult is reading.

Generally, school is divided into three phases: phase one, which might last for three or four years, has to do with learning how to read; phase two is mostly about learning grammar and how you get the words to make sense; and phase three is largely devoted to the use of reading and grammar skills. The subject matter that is not language, like science and social studies, is supportive of language-skill development. All subject areas should teach the child how to think, problem solve, and express ideas clearly.

I think that it's important for a parent to consider what he expects from a school, because then the parent can do a better job understanding the role that he must contribute to the child's education. If you want the school to do the whole job of education, then you have to allow the school all rights to mold and discipline the child as well as to teach the three R's. If, on the other hand, you still see yourself as playing some role in the process, then you must be willing to assume the responsibilities that go along with the job!

Keep an interest in your child's reading: school assignments as well as leisure-time reading. Talk about the selections and offer some help guiding the child toward critical and informative reading. The continuing influence of the home must be felt in the classroom at all times.

Assigned reading in school creates an opportunity for good interaction between parent and child. Make sure that you have read the books that your child is reading because doing so gives you a chance to discuss characters and plots in more than a superficial way. I am not suggesting that you do their work for them, but I am suggesting that you take an informed interest in their work. This doesn't mean that you have to start asking your child's second grade teacher for a book list. Remember, if you keep up the reading at home as I'm suggesting, you will have been exposed to all of those terrific books for the second and third graders anyway. They are books that you may even have read during your own school days. If you haven't read them, you'll enjoy them the first time around, and if you read them twenty years ago, you'll get reacquainted with old friends.

Up to this point I have stressed that it is *never too early to read to your child* and that it is *always too soon to stop.* Reading is a tool the child will use throughout life to gain and to give information. The more that you demonstrate an interest and belief in the habit of reading the greater the chance is that you'll have a reader at home and a student at school.

Your preparation of your child begins with an interest in learning. That interest is supported by reading. It's the reading that provides the background, the information, and the practice that allows the child to meet questions and problems head on.

Effective reading demands a knowledge of language: the meaning of the words and the grammar of the language. You can't understand what you're reading without these two elements. As a parent you need to strengthen both aspects through constant introduction of new words into your child's vocabulary and insistence upon correct usage of language. Reading reinforces these qualities of language through a widening experience with new words and an opportunity to observe skillful use of language. The more exposure that the child has, the greater the familiarity. That's why good readers know a lot. They are regularly exposed to new information clearly presented which sharpens their understanding.

Sometimes, teachers object to the old practice of reading aloud to older students. The objection is based on the concern that schooltime is better spent doing other things. They are often astonished to learn that reading aloud is widely practiced in many European universities, even the best of them. I believe the routine of oral reading allows many advantages, especially for the older student who may, incorrectly, be thought to be skilled at reading and comprehension. Oral reading heightens interest in books, sharpens speaking skills, encourages good listening abilities, and provides an invaluable opportunity for discussion, comprehension, and thinking that rarely exists in many high-school classrooms. It goes a step further by providing a good role model to the student that dignifies reading. This is a practice that should be encouraged.

A teacher I knew had a tenth-grade class of apathetic and undereducated students who had deficient language skills. He decided to try Shakespeare as reading material for the semester. Knowing that many of his students read poorly, he read to them and made Shakespeare come alive for them. Soon the students were enthusiastically participating in the discussions, and most were taking their turn at reading. Today, most of those students still remember the teacher and Shakespeare for developing their willingness to learn and achieve.

Never underestimate the power of reading poetry aloud. This is a practice that is reappearing in many first-grade classes. Even those slow to read efficiently will enjoy poetry, which is easier read and promotes some self-confidence while encouraging comprehension through discussion. Poetry is particularly advantageous for the troubled learner who may stumble over ordinary stories but get through a passage of poetry without as much difficulty (and be a reader to his classmates).

The Troubled Learner

Some children are slower to learn to read and have more difficulty acquiring the skill to use reading effectively. Their disability impairs study skills and increases the effort they must apply to schoolwork for satisfactory achievement. These children can increase efficiency and comprehension while reading if they follow simple rules: isolate specific ideas in the written material and address them separately, organize the pieces into a general idea, and reinforce the material through discussion, outlining, and auditory presentation (tape recorder).

This approach to reading has been used successfully with many children who have trouble with reading comprehension. There are many self-help and remedial reading programs modeled after this method. The important part of the approach is the availability of the parent or teacher to discuss the content of the reading and reinforce the ideas present. Gradually the child learns how to quickly identify the central points about which a paragraph is written.

As these children are "mainstreamed" to keep them in the regular classroom with their peers, they get support, good role models, and even some tutorial assistance from classmates who are better readers. Parents need to continue this effort at home if their child has problems with learning.

Television

It's almost impossible to devote a chapter of this book to reading and not address the topic of TV. Would you believe that the average American child watches more than thirty-six hours of TV a week? That's probably more time in front of the TV set than in front of their teachers and their parents combined.

American fifth graders receive less than twenty hours of school instruction a week; Japanese children receive forty-two hours, plus six more hours of tutoring! They do much better than our children on achievement tests.

We have all read the reports: TV is antisocial, antireading, and antilearning, and it deprives the child of the ability to question, to converse, and to think. It stifles the imagination, promotes a distortion of ordinary life, discourages creativity, and retards learning and reading-skill development. It seems to be the perfect tool to kill the minds of our children. In truth, it has become the primary source of information for most Americans.

Can I say anything good about TV? To me it seems that by its very nature, it's a quick fix that cannot utilize imagination and mental activity. As an information tool it can be used successfully, and as an early learning device for preschoolers it can also be advantageous. It is not a substitute for reading, but unfortunately it has *replaced* reading in many homes.

In our home we never had a problem with TV because our children were too busy doing schoolwork and sports and other activities. There were no restrictions on usage, but we, as parents, were not TV watchers.

I think it's very hard to backtrack and remove something which has become a habit. If kids are used to TV they will yell loudly upon its removal. It's very addictive. There's no question that when you turn the set off, you provide time, activities, and conversation around the home that are absent with a TV set on.

Try the following:

- Encourage family activities, early, that deny time for TV, including relaxed conversation exchange at the dinner table.

- Set an example by reading yourself, and share interesting reading experiences with your child.

- Provide opportunities for enrichment in the arts, sports, crafts, projects, and in other learning situations.

- Expect regular chores and insist upon quality schoolwork.

- Use family excursions to provide an opportunity for time together.

Please note that all of these depend upon *interaction* between parent and child.

Some of our children had favorite TV programs that they occasionally watched. It was never a problem.

Reading is the most important tool that the child acquires during the growing-up years to help develop and use learning abilities. It is also the source of hours of enjoyment that will last through a lifetime.

It's worth repeating: *Good readers are not born, they are made at home.*

Parents often ask for a list of books that their children will enjoy. There is great subjectivity to any list of favorites because tastes differ.

I have listed some of the great books available for children under useful categories like picture books, must-read books, books on tape read by actors, audiotapes and videotapes that are re-creations of classic stories for children. The list is meant as a sample of what's available for the younger child.

BOOK LIST

Picture Books

The Grey Lady and the Strawberry Snatcher, Molly Bang
Pancakes for Breakfast, Tomie De Paola
Naughty Nancy Goes to School, John S. Goodall
Paddy Finds a Job, John S. Goodall
Up and Up, Shirley Hughes
Sleep Tight, Alex Pumpernickel, Fernando Krahn
Frog, Where Are You? Mercer Mayer
The Gift, John Prater
Noah's Ark, Peter Spier
The Happy Dog, Hideyuki Tanaka
Deep in the Forest, Brinton Turkle

Every Child Should Read These Books

Keep Your Mouth Closed, Aliki
The Wonderful Wizard of Oz, L. Frank Baum
Katy and the Big Snow, Virginia Lee Burton
The Very Hungry Caterpillar, Eric Carle
May I Bring a Friend? Beatrice de Regniers

The Story About Ping, Marjorie Flack
Corduroy, Don Freeman
Millions of Cats, Wanda Gag
Bread and Jam for Frances, Russell Hoban
The Snowy Day, Ezra Jack Keats
Lassie Come-Home, Eric Knight
The Carrot Seed, Ruth Krauss
The Story of Ferdinand, Munro Leaf
On Market Street, Anita Lobel
Prince Bertram the Bad, Arnold Lobel
George and Martha, James Marshall
The Little Engine That Could, Watty Piper
Where the Red Fern Grows, Wilson Rawls
Pierre, Maurice Sendak (part of the Nutshell Library)
Brave Irene, William Steig
And to Think That I Saw It on Mulberry Street, Dr. Seuss
Charlotte's Web, E. B. White
Harry, the Dirty Dog, Gene Zion

Poetry

Tomie De Paola's Books of Poems, Tomie De Paola
The Random House Book of Mother Goose, Arnold Lobel
Whiskers and Rhymes, Arnold Lobel
Beneath a Blue Umbrella, Jack Prelutsky
The Random House Book of Poetry for Children, Jack Prelutsky,
    Arnold Lobel
Ride a Purple Pelican, Jack Prelutsky

Videotapes

Abel's Island
The Animal Fables of Leo Lionni, Five Lionni Classics
Anne of Green Gables
Corduroy and Other Bear Stories
Dr. DeSoto and Other Stories

Pecos Bill
The Princess Bride
Ramona
Rebecca of Sunnybrook Farm
Tales of Beatrix Potter
The Velveteen Rabbit, or, How Toys Become Real
Where the Wild Things Are

Audiocassettes of Stories

Madeline, Ludwig Bemelmans
Choo Choo, Virginia Lee Burton
Mike Mulligan and His Steam Shovel, Virginia Lee Burton
The Little Red Hen, Paul Caldone
Corduroy, Don Freeman
Make Way for Ducklings, Robert McCloskey
Lyle, Lyle Crocodile, Bernard Waber

Stories Read by Actors

Beatrix Potter's Stories, read by Claire Bloom.
The Emperor's New Clothes, Jack and the Beanstalk, Nightingale, The Musicians of Bremen, read by Katherine Hepburn
The Velveteen Rabbit, read by Meryl Streep.
Where the Wild Things Are, In the Night Kitchen, The Nutshell Library, read by Tammy Grimes.

10

Creativity

Take time to dream—it's hitching your wagon to a star.

Creativity in the child is his ability to find unusual applications for his knowledge or unusual solutions to ordinary problems. Every child has a certain level of creativity within her awaiting the chance to be developed. Unfortunately much creativity is left undeveloped.

Often we are not very tolerant of kids who do things differently—we don't like surprises. Our society focuses on productivity. Getting things done and doing them in the regular way is usually viewed as the best path. Even our schools contribute to this philosophy. In general, we are more comfortable with standard knowledge. In the face of the rapid changes that occur in our world, just repeating what is already known marks the end of education, not its continuation.

For one reason or another we seem prone to destroy the chance a youngster's native creativity has for reaching the surface. Creativity takes work, and often the creative child isn't too interested in being productive. The creative child, however, shouldn't be an unguided missile. You must help focus and control his creativity.

Earlier in this book I said that failure is an important part of learning. But today we often don't encourage children to take risks, to think differently, even if they might be wrong. This is really at odds with our heritage, for ours is a country built on risk. We were the innovators, the people with the good ideas who were willing to try almost anything. Now we are discouraging our children from this kind of creativity. Some of this is a reflection of insecurity, and some of it flows from the belief that traditional paths are more acceptable.

Henry David Thoreau wrote, "If a man does not keep pace with his companions, perhaps it is because he hears a different drummer. Let him step to the music which he hears, however measured or far away."

A young patient of mine was once asked by his kindergarten teacher to draw a picture of his home. His effort, which filled an entire page and was different from those of his classmates (who drew various shaped boxes), represented the neighborhood in which he lived. He drew his friends' homes, the schoolhouse, and the path they followed each day to arrive at school. To his amazement the teacher criticized his effort since he hadn't done what he was told. I must confess, when I heard of the teacher's response to the child's drawing, I was as surprised as the child. I thought his effort was pretty unusual and insightful for a five-year-old.

Let me clarify creativity as distinct from giftedness in children. It's fair to say that both capabilities are inborn and need to be nurtured. Giftedness is the unusual ability in a child to accomplish a variety of skills early. The gifted child is not only bright and enjoys learning, but his quickness of thought allows him to grasp learning seemingly by instinct. Properly channeled, gifted children often develop particular skills to a high degree of efficiency at a very young age.

We do not ordinarily think of adults as gifted. Instead, we describe the unusually accomplished adult as creative. In fact, there are many highly creative people who were not viewed as particularly gifted during childhood. Albert Einstein is a classic example of a person who fits into that category. Writings about his childhood do not describe him as having unusual abilities, but no one would disagree that a creative genius emerged in adulthood.

Giftedness is an interesting phenomenon in children which, although it occurs infrequently (in less than 1 percent of the population), seems to be a highly desirable trait to many. About 40 percent of the parents of entering kindergarten students believe that their children show unusual talent or some "gifts," while fewer than 5 percent think that their children may have problems learning. Although the percentages are not exactly reversed, the reality is in the other direction. As we've noted, fewer than 1 percent of children are actually gifted. Statistically, more than one child in three will have some problem learning.

Furthermore, gifted children do not necessarily become highly successful and creative adults. This may be a reflection of a variety of circumstances involving home and school that fail to meet the needs of these special children. Our educational system, which tries to be all things for all children, rarely considers these youngsters a priority. In some cases the child's giftedness presents a handicap that must be overcome by the child. I have known several of these child prodigies who in adult life are productive but not out of the ordinary. Occasionally, we find that the brilliant child becomes frustrated dealing with "the rest of us." This frustration can turn into anger, which in turn blurs the focus that is critical in developing the gifted child.

I have treated several gifted children in my practice, only one of whom has done much with the great capability he possessed (he chose the concert stage). Creative children who demonstrate talent in one of many disciplines have been more common in my experience. They are now working at their craft on stage or screen, or in medical laboratories, or even on the sports field. They persevere.

Creativity, which is different from giftedness, is a quality that is always present once it is developed. Creativity manifests itself in change or new understandings of available information. The creative person improves his world by contributing a new way to look at things or by discovering an improved way of doing things. This improvement may be a new medicine, or a better machine, or a faster computer, or a new philosophy.

Creative children do not necessarily excel at school. They may not show the high "intelligence" (that is, perform well on intelligence tests) that characterizes gifted children. Some of this is caused by a lack of conformity and an unwillingness to accept convention. Creative children tend to be critical, challenging accepted ideas.

Little is known of why creativity occurs in one child rather than in another, but let us now put aside the common idea that creativity occurs by magic or suddenly shows up from nowhere. That's a lot of nonsense. A creative child is born with the potential, and there are four conditions that allow the creativity within a child to emerge:

1. Work
2. The development of both sides of the brain
3. Good teachers
4. Encouragement of risk taking

Remember, the focus here is on your child, not on someone else's. Don't make comparisons with other children. If you apply these principles, no matter how carefully, there is no guarantee that you are going to turn your child into a Leonard Bernstein or a Babe Ruth. It means that if the potential is present in your child you're going to help him develop his creativity.

1. *Work* is the willingness to develop the skills to learn what there is to know. It is fundamental to creativity. Creative people, children or adults, are always well informed. This means that you must encourage your child's exposure to the world around her. This exposure is carried out by sharing everyday experi-

ences with your child, talking about them, and getting your youngster involved in learning. This doesn't cost money. It just takes an interest in your child and a willingness to take the time to work with her. When you are in your child's company, no matter how limited that time may be, make it worthwhile.

Why is being well informed such an important part of creativity? The reason is that it's neither creative nor productive to keep reinventing the wheel. You have to know what is known. It's good for children to find out some things on their own, but they shouldn't occupy too much of their time experimenting with things that are already well known. That's where you as their parent and teacher come in. The more they know sooner the greater the likelihood that their time will be spent exploring new information.

2. *The development of both sides of the brain* is crucial to unlocking your child's creativity.

The left side of the brain controls language and the spoken word. The right side is involved in spatial relationships, symbols, and math. If you think about it, much of the emphasis in teaching today is on the left side of the brain, not the right.

As we know, boys are usually better at spatial activities, and girls are usually more verbal than boys. These differences are thought to be related to physical maturity, and it's proposed that girls do schoolwork better because their language functions develop earlier.

One of the concerns educators have raised recently is that too much emphasis in our testing of students involves verbal skills and learning. Teachers generally love students who "participate" in class, not by doing but by saying. For some students the talking is easy, but for others it's painful. The system is set up for the verbal learner.

I am not suggesting that we ignore verbalization—I have already emphasized the importance of verbal learning in the development of the child. In fact, some experts have suggested that the quality of the child's thinking is influenced by his verbal language skills. I am only advocating that the development of the right side of the brain allows the child to learn more easily and more thoroughly. The symbols stored in the right brain often allow us to see things more clearly or to understand them in greater depth.

The great advantage for the child in experiential learning comes from the use of spatial as well as verbal skills. Seeing and hearing reinforces learning. This is particularly true for the creative child who uses visual representation to work through solutions to problems.

3. *Good teachers* are a requirement for every child, and your child's first teacher is you, his parent.

I have always been fascinated by the stories of great men and women and the circumstances that led to their greatness. In an overwhelming number of these people, the greatest influence on their achievements was a parent who led the way, a mother or a father who actively participated in the child's learning experience. Critical to the development of the child was interaction, interest, and inquiry. The parent made it possible for the child to learn, always sharing enthusiasm as well as a love of learning. Often the parent offered interest and enthusiasm without possessing the insight or talent demonstrated by the creative child.

It has often been said that winners of the Nobel Prize usually come from the laboratories of other winners of the Nobel Prize. That precedent underscores the importance of a good learning environment. Educational and psychological research demonstrates that the strongest factors in the education and development of a child come from the child's home.

Take the job of teaching your child seriously. Remember, however, that you are also constantly learning. You may run into a few questions which you cannot answer. Never be afraid to say to your child, "I don't know. Let's find out." Children need good role models. Although they think that their parents know everything, they also respond well to honesty and good direction.

In time, of course, the parent will share the job of teacher with a schoolteacher. That individual must also inspire, guide, and continue to motivate the child. But the critical influence begins at home with the parent. It becomes the joint responsibility of parent and teacher to recognize the creativity in a child and see to it that the talent is developed.

4. *Encouragement of risk taking* is essential if a child is to develop his or her innate creativity.

Risk taking doesn't mean jumping off a building and wondering if you'll hit the ground. It means trying something new that might work and doing so without fear of failure. Failure is part of risk taking. If we always succeed it means we never try anything that's new. Thomas Edison said of ten thousand failures that he never considered them failures but instead saw them as ten thousand ways that didn't work. Without risk there is no creative advancement.

Creative children are inquisitive, usually energetic, and often bothersome because of their enthusiasm. Unfortunately, this is the price of risk taking. The parent must demonstrate a true interest, be patient, trust the child, and not expect that every effort is going to turn out right.

One of my young patients had the privilege of living with his grandfather, who was a great tinkerer, always fiddling with something and trying to improve it. It didn't take long for the child to adopt the interests of the grandfather and begin to add motors to his wagons for improved travel. He had the advantage of a seasoned amateur inventor who supported his interests and tolerated even the wildest of ideas. That's a perfect combination to encourage the creative mind.

Children need the opportunity to think a problem through, try ideas on for size, and enjoy the comfort that support—not criticism—will always be there.

Another element involved in enhancing the creative personality is security, the belief in oneself which I have stressed throughout this book. Each of the qualities which I have set out as necessary to the development of creativity reinforces the child's security.

Creativity in a youngster is built from the ground up. You construct a solid base which will allow creativity to flourish. This will develop in your child a life-style of asking questions and looking for answers. Remember that the creativity is in the child and your job is to allow it to surface. It's like a good pitching arm on a baseball player. The ability lies within but it must be nurtured and encouraged. Keep in mind, however, that you must keep a perspective on things.

One of my medical associates once confided that he had spent perhaps ten years waking up early in the morning to provide opportunity and encouragement for his daughter, a budding ice skater. The girl, although she won her share of figure-skating competitions, by no means ever looked like she was going to become a champion. She was a child who did many things well but none superbly. In the end, it was she who recognized that her future lay down a different path. Today she's a successful lawyer and parent. I'm sure her kids will ice skate better than most.

How do you keep a balance and yet offer a special opportunity? If you keep a child out of the ball park, the Babe Ruth within will never have a chance to emerge.

You have an opportunity to develop an action plan for the creative child who wants to explore a particular talent. Through discussion of problems with other family members obstacles are sometimes brought into focus. Another child within the family may have the opportunity to do some problem solving on his own.

On a late-night talk show I once heard a famous actress/dancer complain about her mother's constant badgering for practice, lessons, and more practice. The actress was quick to admit: no mother, no stardom! The mother must have read the signals properly—the daughter had talent but was inclined to let it go undeveloped because of a lack of discipline. The mother imposed the discipline, and although the immediate effect was unpleasant, it was effective.

This is never an easy job for a parent, and often it is made more difficult because the parent's dreams can get in the way. If you continue to interact with your child you'll read his or her dreams and desires properly. You'll also develop a sense of direction based on an appreciation of your own child's abilities.

A parent should become familiar with his child's abilities. This allows better judgment when deciding what talents to encourage and how. You must make choices for your youngster during the early years so that your child has the options to make his own choices later on.

This brings up another point about creativity in the child: Creativity advances in degrees. It is never all or nothing. Essential to your role in enhancing creativity is that you listen, make time, provide opportunities, focus learning, and encourage and praise.

Up to this point I have been describing the creation of an environment that allows creativity to flourish, one that encourages the child to act as if it's acceptable to be creative.

You may be willing to allow, even encourage, creative behavior, but creativity also implies advancement. True, we don't expect five-year-olds to invent new medicines, but we expect that the lessons learned at five will be applied so that, in time, the child will follow the path of improvement on current knowledge.

There is a second level of activity and concern that must be achieved if the child's creativity is to flower. The second level is where the child must apply his skills. This is where mental discipline is critical, and it is where the child must learn and use the skills of disciplined thought.

To achieve this level the child must learn to approach a problem through organization, evaluation, testing, and application. Remember, creative thought evolves over time. The following elements necessary for functional creative activity need to be taught and applied gradually so as not to discourage the enthusiastic mind.

Organize information. Know what's known and find out how to identify it. This begins in the home or in the local library, and eventually may even lead to the patent office to see if others have attempted a similar project. Next is to state clearly what needs to be accomplished. How are you going to do it? What does the child need to do it? Develop a plan.

Now the plan needs to be carried out. Once done, the child must ask some questions about the result of the plan.

Evaluation of data. Look at the several sides of a problem and ask how it works or why. Would it be better if it were done differently? Learn how to think the project through and make it ready for operation.

Test information. See if it really works better and evaluate if it's practical. This takes work, discipline, and interaction. The child must learn to accept criticism as well as suggestions. Here's where parental support becomes critical. Be sensitive to your child's needs.

Finally, the child must be willing to subject his project to *objective comparison.* Let others, perhaps experts in the field, pass judgment. Remember, creativity means improvement.

These four steps can be applied to art, science, music, or any other creative activity.

Children like to entertain and to be entertained, so keep learning enjoyable. Little children want to go to an animal farm, not a science fair. The day will come when the science fair replaces the animal farm.

Listen, talk, and question children. That's how you get to know them. Don't just make time, make them a part of your world. Keep in mind that you are building a storehouse of experience from which their creative thoughts will flow. How can you talk about oranges if the child has never seen an orange?

Never clutter the child's experience with too much data. Keep a perspective on the child's tolerance for learning.

Not long ago, I sat with two busy professionals who were worried about their child and his development. They expected too much too soon. They also went about encouraging him in the wrong way. They planned too much, bought too many toys, and spent far too little time with him. Their relationship with their child was never enjoyable. I don't think they liked the child—he was a disappointment to them. They wanted a creative child, but they were trying to buy one. It doesn't work that way. The child's needs were simple: fewer things and more interaction with his parents.

Today, many parents must rely on day-care centers to provide the stimulation and activities that will lead to creative play in their children. Sometimes this is not easy, but it is not impossible. Make sure that the staff gets their hands into the job. You need to see that the day-care program will continue to provide the opportunity for your child that exists at home. That's an important part of its job.

Notice that I shy away from "creative" toys as useful playthings or activities for children. Some of them are excellent. Often, however, they are substitutes for an involved parent. There is no substitute for your interaction with your child.

How do you make time for children? This is a frequently asked question today when so many parents are working. The answer is simple: let your children participate in your activities at every opportunity. Give them helping jobs and make them part of your life at home. Plan activities that will offer them exposure as well as entertainment.

Stop for a moment and think of all the things that must be done around the house, uncreative jobs that can stand a little creativity. These include everything from washing dishes to washing clothes. Children need to learn that they are part of your world and that a family is a cooperative effort. Everybody has a job. Being needed reinforces security.

After you make time, make opportunity. This opportunity should exist at home, at the child-care center and outside the home, whether in excursions or at school.

Kids need safe areas at home to play on their own with dolls or trucks or with crayons and paintbrushes. You don't need a toy store or a computer at home to create a play area. You need a little thought. A place for a child to explore or build takes very little expense, as do coloring books and paints. Children also need special places where they can retreat to, to think or to dream.

Creative children must have the opportunity to let their imaginations run wild. This usually means time separated from group activities. Don't make them apologize or feel uncomfortable when they want to retreat to their special place.

In your interactions with your child gradually provide an increasing amount of complex experiences. Children must have the opportunity to stretch their imaginations. This demands experience as well as the chance to discuss ideas that arise from these experiences.

Learning must be focused. This is particularly true for children. Creative kids can, in their enthusiasm, jump from one area of interest to another. Each area generates a new flood of questions. Don't discourage the questions, but do encourage sticking to one idea at a time. Offer help as needed. When the child realizes that you're listening she will focus more.

Nothing discourages a parent more quickly than endless questions from an enthusiastic youngster. In turn, nothing discourages a child more than a parent who is not listening. The answer is to turn creative distraction into creative production.

A little praise goes a long way with children. Actually, everyone needs a pat on the back, but children thrive on encouragement. If the praise is properly placed it guides the youngster to continue a particular path. When a youngster brings you work that needs help, focus your attention on the problem. This is a strong message to the child: I care. Sometimes it's necessary to say, "I will help you with that after supper." Make sure that you do what you say.

Children can be organized without a put-down. I often hear parents say, "Never mind your silly ideas, John, just come to dinner." Artists start with a line, not the completed picture. The same can be said for any creative work or idea. Children who are introducing an original idea need support, not criticism. They are usually very sensitive.

Youngsters need to realize that some wild thought or interest can be shaped into a useful idea, but that mental discipline must be involved. This is hard work and demands patience. The parent needs to think the project through and encourage the child to think. Insist that the youngster work at her ideas with your support. Let the child explain the idea from her point of view. Then help her refine it.

Mental discipline means order; without it learning is unproductive. This is hard for us to teach our children because many of us struggle with it ourselves.

It's an important lesson for a child to learn that discipline often amounts to boring repetition. Athletes and scientists alike learn this fact of discipline.

If we take a child by the hand and help him pick up toys, imposing a routine that we are willing to apply until it is learned, then we have begun the job of discipline. Add a pleasurable reward, such as a bedtime story, after the job is done and it will become automatic sooner. Children love to please parents, but unfortunately many parents undermine their own efforts with inconsistent behavior.

Discipline should not mean rigidity or doing things without applying some common sense. I think of mental discipline as orderly sensible behavior. It must be based on solid information, yet allow enough freedom to look at the various sides of a problem.

Some cultures thrive on work while others regard creativity as most important. Japanese fifth-graders go to school twice as long each day as their American counterparts. These youngsters acquire facts, mental discipline, and good grades. Learning is linked to family honor but also to economic success. Competition is important. Creative activity is not encouraged because the immediate rewards may not be great.

The American child by contrast has been allowed a tradition of exploration of new ideas and creativity, and his parent respects and fosters his independence. The parent also focuses on concepts, not procedures. The idea of developing creativity in our children is sound. It allows the child the opportunity to improve life through creative endeavors. Unfortunately, the steps to achieve creative activity have been abandoned. We don't need to discard the plan, we need to implement it. Creativity demands hard work, and the child must be prepared for it.

The preparation for the discipline and work that underlie creative activity must occur during the apprenticeship years with the family in the home. But the family, in many instances, has fallen apart, and this denies care and training usually afforded children during development. We have sent our children's first teachers (mothers) off to the workplace and to date we haven't replaced them. We expected, naively, that learning would go on as usual. This isn't true. We're also finding out that creativity in children doesn't happen by magic. It emerges through solid preparation, loving care, and continued hard work.

Good ideas need to be tested to see if they work. Get your child into the habit of informed experimentation. This means trying out ideas and getting rid of the bad ones. It starts at home with you. Kids need to work at problems and think through solutions. Persistence is an important characteristic of the creative mind. No one solves a tough problem immediately. Sometimes solutions evolve over years, one step at a time.

A lot of people have written about a child's need to have time of her own. This is very important for the evolution of creativity. Kids need the time to think, to let dreams take shape and grow. Parents must provide opportunities and support. They also need to be there as a sounding board for the child's ideas, holding judgment until the child's mind has had time to play with the idea. Find out about the child's interests and explore them with her. Help her explore new resources so that she is encouraged to continue exhaustive inquiry.

You must believe in your kids if they are to become creative. Each child has unique strengths and weaknesses. Your job is to nurture the strengths while supporting the weaknesses so that, as changes in development occur, you have prepared your child to make the most of his talents.

Creativity always demands change, something new that improves upon the old. This takes time, perseverance, and the skills to work out the solution that creates the change.

Unfolding within this book is an intricate mix of functions that contribute to the emergence of the whole child. This mix begins with love, and each function within its own place and time is nurtured by the interaction between child and parent. As security, socialization, and verbalization strengthen the beginnings of this effort, and enrichment expands the job, reading and discipline insure fulfillment. Creativity, and all that it embodies—independence, risk, and the desire to improve things—is the end product of this integrated child.

The evolution of creativity in the child only occurs with a lot of hard work, order, and patience. There's no magic to its development. The magic is in its expression.

11

Discipline

Take time to work—it's the price of success.

Parents have more problems with discipline then with any other child-rearing activity. There are several reasons for this. Discipline involves consistency, follow-through, and fairness. Most of all, however, it involves an understanding of the objectives of discipline and the true meaning of the word. Discipline is an act of teaching which comes from love and concern for the child.

Disciplining children must involve four different aspects: concern, teaching, control, and punishment. In each instance the activity should focus on the child and be an act of caring. The action of the child must be the objective of discipline, and the parent must learn how to modify that action for the child's sake.

The parent's approach to the administration of discipline has some far-reaching effects on the parent-child relationship and influences, in some situations, how the child will deal with adult relationships in the future.

It is your primary responsibility to teach your child the order and control that will govern how he will approach various life situations. It is equally important that he exercise some control over his own behavior and limit excessive responses so there is a balance to his life. In both cases, discipline is being imposed. In all cases it should be imposed with love.

Punishment is what many people have in mind when they discuss discipline. Just the other day on a talk show I heard a discussion about parents who were frustrated by the advice they had received from their doctors about punishment and control of their children. Each parent had returned to spanking his or her children with what he or she considered good results. Recently I read that although most parents disapprove of spanking children in school, many resort to it at home.

If you are a child who has been punished by physical force, when you encounter an adult you think will strike you at best you learn to duck and at worst you lose any respect that you might have had for that person. In some cases you get angry.

Now take the case of the child who looks at his parents with respect and love. This love translates into security, which provides the child with a base for normal development. As a parent you are responsible for teaching and guiding your child during the formative years. You are also responsible for the care and safety that must be part of her life. She must respect you in order to create the relationship that must exist if discipline is going to work.

There are several questions you must consider in the application of discipline: Is the focus of the correction on helping the child? Is the parent's action a response to her threatened authority? Is the motivation for discipline love and improved development rather than punishment for wrongdoing?

The parent's approach to the child is based on how he views the child's action and on his own response to it. A parent may use punishment and control or may use affection and caring as the basis for discipline. One approach is autocratic while the other is authoritative. The second implies helping rather than manipulation. Children don't want to be browbeaten and they don't want to be forced. They resent control because it threatens their sense of individuality, of being people distinct from others.

Your means of achieving control and establishing limitations has to begin with self-control in yourself. That's often the reason discipline becomes physical punishment; in the rush or frustrations of the day parental self-control is often lost. We lose patience and we get angry. We may even feel insecure about our child-rearing capabilities. But the child looks on you as a model, someone who is not supposed to fall apart. If you crumble, you shake his sense of security and create an atmosphere of uncertainty.

Maybe life would be pretty dull on the home front if we were all models of self-control, just quietly going about life. Certainly kids don't act that way. They are full of enthusiasm, with wide swings in behavior that sometimes make the whole business of self-control seem impossible. But the greatest problem we experience in the control of our children is our own inconsistency and lack of self-discipline.

The key to self-control in the child lies in the child's respect for the parent as well as in the parent's own self-control. Its maturation takes time and requires patience on the part of the parent.

The parent who loves and cares for the child is the role model. His behavior sets the example for the child, but often this painstaking process is slow to evolve in the parent (let's reflect on our own childhoods!). It is not unusual for the parent to be impatient with the development of this control in himself as well as in the child. The parent wants perfection now. He wants to be able to see the changes immediately. Often he is trying to develop this in the child when it hasn't developed in himself. But life with children doesn't work that way, and the job is just as slow and painstaking in them. Sometimes we forget that time and patience are key factors in discipline.

Do you ever wonder how some parents seem to enjoy such control and respect? They appear to have a hassle-free life with their kids. We know from studies done in the past that if we are in control and our children love us they'll imitate us without any excessive urging. It just happens in a natural fashion. Children don't want to be viewed as bad guys by their parents. They want and need ongoing approval and security. Life works better for them that way.

Discipline comes in different packages. The seriousness of the problem is always a matter of how different parents look at different situations. Some parents insist that their child say good morning to the nursery school teacher or come to the dinner table with clean hands, while other parents don't care as much about manners. Other parents want to prevent their child from riding his bike on busy streets that pose physical dangers. The response to infractions of family rules is more or less severe depending upon the seriousness of the problem as perceived by the parent. Sometimes this can be confusing to a child who may not understand why her friend's parent gave the friend a lecture while she got a spanking from her own parent.

Parents do interesting things to discipline children. They offer praise or punishment, reward or denial, approval or criticism, even dispense love or withdraw it. Some rely heavily upon physical force while others use love, positively or negatively, as the approach to discipline. Sometimes parents turn a good strategy for learning into one that has negative effects.

The parent who needs to get her three-year-old into bed (for the third time that evening) has to exercise some problem solving. This can be intellectual, although reasoning with a three-year-old is not likely to work; psychological, such as threats; or physical, which will work if properly applied. If the parent carries the child to bed, which can be done with either anger or laughter, it may signify physical control to which the child objects. If, on the other hand, the parent applies a desirable alternative to remaining up, such as a bedtime story, the plan will work.

Gentle persuasion will work with a child if you know your child and your child respects you.

The other day, I saw a seven-year-old in the office who had resisted coming. The father was "understanding," creating an environment of help while offering that the child "wouldn't want to disappoint him, would she?" The father placed a price tag on approval. The mother, on the other hand, was more angry. She laid guilt trips on the child. "Does she know how much this costs? Does she understand what medicines cost?" The child didn't know what the mother was talking about, but she knew that she had the upper hand. The child reacted predictably by playing one parent against the other. She cried and refused to cooperate.

The one thing you must have to apply discipline is agreement between parents.

Parents need to think twice before initiating discipline. If force or physical punishment is used, the child will become resentful, angry, and, in all likelihood, aggressive. This creates aggression between parent and child that eventually leads to distrust and dislike between the two. The antagonism that develops can be threatening to the child and impair the emergence of sound moral values in the youngster. Right or wrong is supplanted by control.

The use of affection as a tool for handling discipline can be equally troublesome. Children want to be loved, they need to be loved. When a parent threatens to withdraw this love as a means of discipline, it sends a message of withdrawal of support. This has a great impact on the child. It creates dependency and a loss of self-esteem. It interrupts independence and eventually creates distrust.

Many parents lack confidence in their child-rearing practices and need to demonstrate control. The anxiety created by this sense of inadequacy causes them to exert control where they think it will have an effect. Exerting control, however, can backfire.

Other problems that absolutely destroy discipline are the "Do as I say not as I do" approach and the "Do it because I tell you to do it" approach. After the first few years, children normally do not respond very well to orders from a parent who simply says to do something without an explanation. The parent will have lost those valuable first years of training when the foundations of discipline should have been laid. I'm not saying that you should sit down and try to arrive at a democratic solution to a problem caused by your three-year-old daughter. Some parents overdo such shared responsibility programs, too. The most effective way to handle problem situations is to be firm, listen carefully, and then act. Kids need to know that someone they respect is in charge. They also need to know the limits and the consequences attached to ignoring them. That reinforces security, which in turn makes discipline work.

Punishment without explanation is usually resented, often loses the instructive value intended, and therefore is ineffective. Clarify what the discipline is all about.

If you ask a child to wash for dinner and, through fooling around, something valuable is broken by the child, your anger at the loss will not be understood unless explained. If you don't explain, the child will wonder why dinner or clean hands are so important.

Dictatorships don't work any better in the home than they do outside. If someone else runs your life you may bend to the moment but it does not necessarily mean that you've learned anything. It only means that you see no way out for the time being. Just as soon as you see an opportunity to avoid the rule you'll take advantage of it. You're bending to authority for one reason or another, but you're not learning self-control. In fact, you may be fighting it, storing up anger to lash out when the chance presents itself.

That's not discipline. That's physical or mental control. That's what you usually get with punishment. The child bends to the wishes of the parent just as long as the parent is bigger than he. Sooner or later the big question asked is "How are you going to make me?" Then the parent has lost the opportunity to teach, to show concern, and to teach control.

I repeat: Discipline should be a learning rather than a punitive action.

Did you ever wonder how some situations deteriorate to the point where the child bullies the parents or calls all of the shots?

The irony is that such children want and need to be told what to do and reassured that they are going to be made to do it. They are crying out for limits.

Discipline in a child is an outgrowth of love and concern that creates a mutual respect between parent and child. Self-control is founded on this respect and it is the first rule of discipline.

The second rule is that physical punishment never taught anyone anything except perhaps that big people can inflict harm on little people. The end result is always resentment, not learning, self-control, or discipline.

Never focus on the child when his wrongdoing causes disapproval. Instead, focus on the event or the wrongdoing itself.

Never humiliate the child.

Never cause resentment or anger.

Never lessen the child's self-esteem.

Never strike the child.

Never tell a child that she isn't loved.

Keep in mind that children are real people. Never assume that they are always wrong and never deny them the opportunity to express their side of the story. In general, kids act at any moment in the belief that what they are doing is best for them at the time, even if they are wrong. If they have done wrong, they need to learn what they've done wrong and what should have led them to a different decision.

Build respect early with love and caring. True, some kids are headstrong, but all respond to love.

Use their names, get their attention, and keep control, of yourself as well as of the child.

Try to be consistent and follow through. If you let the situation slip away you're going to get frustrated or angry and end up doing something you'll regret later.

There will be times when you decide to take your child to some public place where she will run amok. You may lose control, yell and fuss, spank her, and retreat, angry with the whole situation. Mostly you'll be angry with yourself for allowing this to happen.

These situations, usually, have been created long before the day on which they happen. Step back and examine the situation. Ask yourself how you might have done things differently.

Look at your own follow-through at home. Do you ordinarily practice control of a situation on the home front?

When you say something do you see to it that it gets carried out?

Should your child have been with you at that time? Was the situation appropriate?

When you say no to him, do you mean it? Can you enforce the no if you must?

Do you allow the child too much freedom at first and then expect by magic that she's going to reverse her behavior?

Are you being realistic with him in public? Are you realistic with him at home?

Are you consistent with your child?

Inconsistency causes confusion and intensifies anger and hostility in the child. If you're going to develop discipline, then you need to offer some predictable behavior for her to build on.

Sometimes I think those of us who see children in our offices could use some of our own advice. We schedule children for appointments, make them wait longer than they should (creating anxiety and fatigue in the parent), and then everyone involved is upset by misbehavior in the child.

There are issues that initiate the need for disciplining children: eating, safety, respect for belongings, control of aggression, social adherence, school achievement, and respect for parents. Some of these have to do with the child while others have to do with the parent. In some instances the perceived needs of the child create concern that demands action.

Parents are instructed through their doctor, family members, or reading that a routine of good nutrition must be followed to insure the health of the child. Their own needs are superimposed on the child's so that a schedule must be met and a diet must be followed by the child. This is the first encounter with discipline. Other demands, such as safety, will follow. Often this creates a confrontation between parent and child. Such confrontation is not bad. Children need to learn how to exercise assertive or aggressive behavior in an acceptable way. You don't want the child to become so passive that he avoids all confrontation. This leaves him without the necessary self-image to handle life events.

Occasionally, I will see children who think and act through their parents. This situation is created by a parent who refuses to tolerate disagreement. His point of view is always correct. Naturally, the child becomes submissive and loses all sense of identity. Healthy disagreement, properly defended, is a desirable step in the evolution of the child's personality. This aggression must be tempered in the social encounters that will soon occupy much of his developmental years. It is a critical part of the acquisition of self-regulation.

We have discussed earlier that kids have reasons for tossing things around. However, they need to learn that certain objects at home will not withstand being tossed around. This begins the respect for "things" that will lead to self-control and a respect for others. This control must be extended to a personal discipline that is necessary for properly maintaining one's belongings, carrying out helping chores, and in doing schoolwork. From this comes pride in achievement, pride in home, and pride in oneself.

It goes without saying that discipline underlies achievement at home, in school, and on the sports field.

We have all witnessed the child who, upset by a bad shot on the sports field, throws a bat or a racquet in disgust. Unsportsmanlike behavior begins early in the child with the failure to acquire personal discipline during the preschool years.

There is a prevalent need, and certainly an expectation, that children offer respect and will show obedience (when demanded) to their parents. This takes discipline that focuses on the parent's needs. The imposition of this notion of expected behavior must begin early and should be reinforced often. How is it, then, that we see many children, particularly today, who show no obedience or respect for their parents? What went wrong? Most of these problems arise out of three failures during child rearing: mixed messages between parent and child, inconsistency from the parent, and a lack of respect from the parent for the child. Discipline in the child must be built on mutual respect between parent and child.

I cannot stress too strongly that discipline is an act of caring. It depends upon mutual respect, a good role model in the parent, and a need for parent and child to feel part of the family. Also, remember that discipline is an evolving process, one that takes time to emerge. Three-year-olds cannot be fully disciplined. Ultimately, discipline is an act of control that benefits both the parent and the child, and that's why it's built on love.

Children need discipline in order to function properly in life. A family is a cooperative effort and every child has a place, even a job, in the effort. But families are not democracies. Parents are the leaders who ideally listen carefully to both sides and are willing to make judgments and see them through to completion. Discipline takes practice. You have to do it regularly to make it work.

As all of us parents know, it's not easy to get a preschooler to keep toys where they belong or to put soiled clothes in the hamper. Is it hard work to instill that kind of training in the child? You bet it is, and at times you'll be convinced that this kid doesn't know how to learn. It gets worse, however, if you don't begin early and treat it seriously. You must get the child into a routine of jobs around the house as soon as it's practical. Life is going to be a problem if you have skipped this part of her upbringing. Children should get used to jobs and responsibilities, and home is the place to start.

A family is a miniature society that demands give-and-take. This is why it is so appropriate to instill discipline within the context of the family. The ordinary demands of that society need discipline. This is a cooperative effort, and participation requires a respect for the rights of others.

Work and responsibilities at home teach the child how to use time effectively and how to get results. Many parents today need all of the help that they can get from their youngsters, and their children need the experience.

The old adage about child rearing still applies: Do for them, help them do, watch them do, and then let them do. But do they must.

Children need to develop and assume some pride in themselves, in their family and home, in the quality of their work, and in the quality of their general behavior. This pride comes from discipline.

Almost everything that a child does involves some degree of discipline—schoolwork, sports, home life, even a job outside of the home in later years. In fact, there is no human endeavor that can be accomplished successfully without discipline. It is crucial, then, that parents begin instilling discipline in their children early and make sure that discipline goes on forever. Discipline is the price of success, and success is worth the price.

12

The Troubled Learner

Take time to laugh—it's the music of the soul.

Children have problems learning for many reasons—some have neurological problems that resulted from birth injury and some have emotional difficulties that interfere with the learning process. There are other children who are born with subtle abnormalities, imperfectly understood, that interfere with the normal learning process. Some of these children have dyslexia, others have attention deficits, while still others have difficulties interpreting what they see or hear. For nearly twenty-five years I have worked professionally with these youngsters.

Learning Disabilities

In the 1960s most professionals argued that children with learning disabilities didn't exist or that the problems were overstated. As late as the 1970s some university education departments were arguing that there were no such things as dyslexia or learning disabilities.

Eventually parents of learning disabled children made enough noise that schools and state education departments were forced to pay attention. In truth, all the parents were asking was that educators treat the troubled learner fairly and see that he or she get an education like all the rest of the children.

When I was growing up, you did what you were told in school, and each class ended with assigned homework. The contract was between you and the teacher. Parents showed up once in a while to meet the teachers. No parent had much influence on the way the school was run or what his child did in class. The teacher was the boss. Of course, mistakes were made, injustices occurred, and sometimes kids were treated unfairly, but that was the system. You had to work, you learned respect quickly, and there were consequences for all of your actions.

Ironically, troubled learners did pretty well in that system because of its rigid structure, not because anyone knew what they needed. For many years these children received tutorial assistance to get them through their classes, but no one knew, or at least not many knew, why they needed the help.

Along came the 1960s and schools responded to the idea that children learn best in an environment that supports their interest (which happens to be true). Our educational system introduced the concept of "open classrooms" where self-guidance on the part of the student dictated the curriculum. Apparently, educators hoped that their sheer enthusiasm would make children into good students. Open classrooms, however, were a disaster waiting to happen. Children who are having trouble learning to read are rarely motivated to do something that they have difficulty doing. They are more likely to go off and play with the gerbils.

Under the old system, teachers had a fighting chance when everyone in class was doing the same thing. With open classrooms teachers had to shift gears all day long to respond to twenty or twenty-five youngsters, each of whom was likely to be doing something different. Hand in hand with this new system was a loosening of the discipline that had characterized the pre-1960s classroom.

About the same time, recognition of learning problems
emerged and programs to meet the needs of learning disabled
children were mandated. This special education for troubled
learners required a new curriculum and new training for the
teachers.

With the onset of "special education" and the chaos that
followed, parents soon became active participants in their children's curriculum development. Roles were reversed so that now
the school and teacher had to get the parent's approval to
institute a special course of instruction for his or her troubled
learner. As was often the case, neither parents nor teachers knew
what to do with children who needed "special education." The
experts, whether psychologists or physicians, were not very
expert, and often bad advice was piled on bad advice.

In my own early experience I found that much advice was
aimed at emotional therapy, particularly if the expert was a
psychologist or psychiatrist. Teachers, on the other hand, went
through a phase of recommending "perceptual training," that is,
copying geometric designs or learning to sequence sounds or
visual symbols. This approach was thought to help learning
disabled children read better.

Special private schools, mostly with a watered-down basic
curriculum, a slower pace, and in some instances a structured
program with fewer students per teacher, appeared and disap-
peared. In most cases these schools were very expensive and were
highly dependent upon state funding for survival. As the money
dried up, so did the special schools. In truth, the public schools
fought against special education until it hurt their pocketbooks,
then they joined the movement, replacing the need for the special
private school. Today a relatively small number of the private
programs survive. They are an available option for the parent
who can afford them. Many of the traditional private schools
have found that their survival is dependent upon providing for
the needs of all students, even the troubled learners.

The widespread practice of depending on the school to correct the problem of these youngsters has not been as successful as once thought. Studies have shown that the most successful programs for the troubled learner are ones that focus on home as well as school, with the greater emphasis on home. This doesn't mean that the child's program at school can ignore his problem, but it does stress the critical element of a supportive home life.

Years ago, an associate of mine who was a psychologist thought it would be a good idea if we offered the parents of children attending a special school an opportunity to meet with us and talk about home management. The parents thought it was a great idea, but their concerns were about the children getting dressed faster in the morning, doing homework without prodding, and limiting TV watching. The teachers thought we were assuming some of their job. How often we ran into that kind of resistance! Much time was wasted during those early years trying to convince teachers that our shared information might help the child. We thought our efforts should be aimed at getting the kids to believe in themselves and to look at life positively, not negatively.

For years, professionals wrote countless articles and speeches about the different "profiles" of children who had trouble learning. The idea was that the children saw things backward. Some of them did. Recently I came across a paper done by one of my sons in first or second grade with perfect mirror writing.

In fact, I have dyslexia. When I was in the Navy I was assigned to a job where I drew the course of our ship on a lighted table map so that the officers in command knew where the various ships in our convoy were. The officers got to look at the map right side up while I, as an enlisted man, had to do my drawing upside down and backward. I never had any trouble doing that and many officers were amazed that it looked so readable. I always knew that my dyslexia would pay off.

Although I believe strongly that everyone needs to learn how to read and write in a literate society, reading and writing make up only a small piece of the picture in troubled learners. Most experts view them as children with reading problems. This is an incomplete understanding of the problem, and sometimes this limited idea causes incomplete management of the difficulty.

We have learned two things about these children that have a strong influence on what we do with them in their formative years. First, the problem never goes away—you don't outgrow it, and learning how to read or write doesn't cure the problem. This means that the child has to accommodate the problem early through the development of special learning strategies and then use these learning skills as he approaches any new problem. It's like the good golfer who goes through a set routine to line up every shot. If he's careless, the shot doesn't work.

The second thing that we've learned about these children is that their lack of self-confidence is what hurts them most in their lifetime activities. That's why I stress the need for expressing love, praise, and reinforcement.

This brings up some of the characteristics that haunt troubled learners throughout life:

1. they don't believe in themselves. They have no confidence in their ability, so they shy away from participation.
2. They anticipate failure, which, because of their problem, often occurs.
3. They avoid risks because they don't want to fail again. This further limits learning.
4. They need constant stroking, which becomes tiresome to everyone in their environment. This in turn affects how well they mix or get along with others. Children and adults avoid those who need praise all of the time.

Children who lack confidence expect to fail, avoid anything new or challenging, and offer constant excuses for not trying. Even when they excel they still find it hard to get involved. Their lives are filled with fear and anxiety that can become crippling to them. Some of the special school programs reinforce the insecurity through individual attention. When children leave the school program they discover that the real world doesn't respond that way. That's why instruction and training by the parent is essential.

One of my earliest patients was a bright child with dyslexia who had many natural gifts. He was good at sports, he could draw well, and he had a talent for music. He didn't read or write until he was in the fourth grade and he expected to fail. Peter was quick to please and he had unusual social graces for a child his age. Most people thought he was great, and out of school he was everyone's favorite. Despite all of the praise that he received, Peter viewed himself as a loser. He struggled through school, but everyone was cheering for him when he graduated. One-on-one Peter was terrific; in a crowd he withdrew. College was not successful for him because he got lost in the crowd. After college he worked at sales positions, each of which was less demanding than the previous one. He has gradually assumed a role in life where there are no expectations of him. Despite all of his talent, Peter doesn't believe in himself. This lack of self-esteem has him paralyzed.

Children need self-esteem. And they need to succeed to build that self-esteem. The troubled learner doesn't believe in himself, and therefore doesn't believe that he can succeed. To compensate, he argues that it doesn't matter if you succeed. It's hard work convincing himself that success doesn't matter. The frustration can be hard on the child and even worse on the family.

As a troubled learner, you set the stage through a lack of confidence and an unwillingness to get involved to become someone who is hard to get along with, tends to listen poorly, and often attempts to bolster a sagging ego by becoming a know-it-all. None of these characteristics is particularly desirable to family or friends.

Conversely, I have had patients who have had severe problems with their learning, but overcame their handicaps through hard work and a belief in themselves. Matt was a learning disabled child of a single parent who worked hard at everything he did. The support from his mother was unusual. Through a scholarship he attended a prestigious school and did solid B work. He had two dreams for college: the Naval Academy or Harvard. Although I cautioned him about the unusual competition for admission at each of those schools, he was determined and ultimately convinced the admissions office at Harvard that he would be an asset. Hard work and solid home support pays off.

The underlying problem of the troubled learner is one of an inability to understand or interpret either visual or auditory information. This means that the child has difficulty learning his letters or sounds, reads more slowly, and probably writes badly. As I've said before, in a society where you have to communicate with others just to get by, the troubled learner is denied the opportunity to learn things about life because he lacks the appropriate skills for language. The child is the first one to appreciate that he doesn't know things. It's hard to fool yourself!

One of my patients who had a learning disability attended a summer math class to make up for the course that he failed during the year. Frank was angry when the teacher gave him a B. When I asked why he thought he deserved better he replied, "Not better, I should have flunked. I didn't learn anything and the teacher didn't care. Someday I may need that information." Frank was right. The teacher had no right giving him a B in a course that he should have flunked. Frank was also right to be angry. If school is a meaningless ritual, why did the teacher flunk him in the first place?

There's another problem that often occurs in the child who has a learning problem: the youngster is underinformed. Because of her disability, she is denied access to the usual information— whether it's book learning or street sense—that a child of her age acquires. This lack of exposure is magnified by the child's poor ability to get the whole picture or read the social signals that are available. Often these youngsters cannot generalize, so they pick away at specifics that may be irrelevant to the point at issue. These kids may not get the point of a joke easily because they need things carefully explained to them. They are usually quite literal. Worse, they respond poorly in a social setting because they lack the ability to pick up the signals being offered. Their underinformed or inappropriate behavior may cause them to be the butt of jokes. Their friends may erroneously think that they are dumb. Because of this, the troubled learner may eventually avoid her playmates.

Why is the family so important to these children?

Simply put, the family exerts its influence all of the time, and these kids need reinforcement all of the time. I've spoken about interaction throughout this book. That means getting your child involved in his world. It's never too early.

Think of the word LOVE.

L is for the love that you must show your child as well as the love of learning. Be inquisitive yourself and encourage inquisitiveness in your child.

O is for opportunity. One of the best reasons for early involvement with your youngster in the learning process is that exposure to ordinary life situations is the best way for the troubled learner to acquire knowledge. This is learning by experience.

V is for verbalization. When you interact with your child you give him the benefit of what you know, and you find out what he knows. This is an important step in the learning process.

E is for enrichment, which means new experiences of any kind. It's easy to remember something if you've experienced it. This is very important for the youngster who has trouble connecting facts or information.

The better you get to know your child's abilities the more easily you recognize that help is needed. When I was working on the BASICS child development project, which is a program, written for use in the home and the professional office, aimed at helping parents recognize and enhance the abilities of their three- to eight-year-old children, some psychologists objected that the more parents knew about their children's abilities (or needs) the more anxious they became. This was not only nonsense, it baffled me. For years teachers and school psychologists believed that if only they could get to these children earlier they could do a good job with them. Anxiety is created by a lack of understanding, not by knowledge. The earlier that you understand that your child needs help, the earlier you are likely to provide it.

The Hyperactive Child

No one is more aware of her child's needs than the mother of a hyperactive child.

I was asked once if I'd participate in a study of hyperactive preschoolers. One of the requirements for the parents was that they participate in group sessions to talk about their problems and what they did to overcome their concerns. For the parents this was probably the best part of the study. I think we saved a few families from divorce by getting both parents involved with the child. And importantly, we got the school where these children were in attendance, wherever possible, involved with the child to help him through the early learning steps. None of the children in the study had any major difficulties with schooling because the support was early and effective.

In medicine and in education the hyperactive child has been a major subject of study and concern for years. Wiggly Willie is a character in an old German nursery rhyme from the 1700s, so we are certain that recognition of the phenomenon is not new. Hyperactivity in children may be the result of brain dysfunction, some subtle injury, or even an inherited problem. In most cases, the cause is poorly understood.

When a neurologist working with mildly brain damaged children observed that central stimulants, like dexedrine, seemed to quiet these youngsters, some drug companies got into the "pep pill" business. The most economically successful of these pills has been Ritalin, a drug that has become such big business that the federal government now regulates how much can be produced. Which, by the way, is far less than the demand.

In the 1960s Ritalin was called "smart pills" since hyperactive kids were made manageable in the classroom, thus allowing learning to take place.

Most vivid in my mind is a classroom I visited in a suburban Boston community. Eight youngsters, aged eight to ten, were in the room, some under the desks, others trying to snare goldfish for lunch, while a well-meaning teacher operated a movie camera showing a film about the human heart. Between her tears even she saw the humor in the situation. Common sense would have dictated that these youngsters be separated from one another into a controlled and less active environment.

Even today, as appalling as it may seem, some parents are told to get their child on central stimulants before he can return to school.

Ironically, the medical profession associates hyperactivity with learning problems and thus endorses the use of stimulant drugs in children. Some doctors focus their professional lives on the use of pep pills in children, and many doctors continue to prescribe central stimulants like aspirin. In many cases the parent is instructed to increase the dose until the child is quiet, without concern for side effects. And the side effects of central stimulants are very real. Some kids get spooky, some hallucinate, some stop growing, many say they feel weird, and some lose control while on the drugs. I've always asked if it seems reasonable to put a child on pep pills.

One of the problems with the hyperactive child is that he is out of control. Both parent and child need to know that control is possible. Drugs offer that control quickly, thus their appeal to some parents and to some teachers. Behavior modification through gentle arms around the child takes patience, time, and follow-through. This may be easy in some settings but not so easy in an active home.

In my earlier years, I turned a country estate into a summer program for troubled learners. We accepted perhaps one hundred children for a learning experience that blended camp with school. The children came to improve their learning skills. This

was accomplished by a large staff that offered individual attention, caring, and an understanding of the problem in the
children that limited their school performance. Many of the
children were on pep pills when they arrived at the camp. We
requested parental and physician approval to reduce the dosage
or discontinue the pep pills in the children as soon as possible.
We thought the large staff and the environment would exercise
control of the children's behavior without the pills. Two weeks
into the program, only an occasional child was on medication at a
fraction of the dose. Environmental control works, but takes
effort.

There is also a great deal of variability among parents in their
tolerance for active children. I was visiting my son's second-
grade classroom one day and in the middle of some exercises he
mounted an imaginary motorcycle and vroom-vroomed his way
around the class. When the motorcycle was apparently safely at
rest and my son had resumed his chair his teacher asked if he had
had a nice ride. In my day you can bet that a less tolerant teacher
would have had more to say about that morning ride.

Today we refer to these children as having an *attention deficit
disorder*, with or without hyperactivity.

For some time there was a popular notion that linked junk
food, excessive sugar, and food dyes to hyperactivity. Despite a
lot of fans who believed strongly, the evidence could not withstand careful scientific scrutiny. It was suggested that the parent
in managing the child's diet added an element of control that
acted to create behavior modification. Recently, however, some
research has indicated that hyperactive people metabolize sugar
in their brains differently.

We do know that learning is a form of decision making and
that the child must be an active participant in the process if she's
going to learn anything. Hyperactive kids don't pay attention
consistency. Usually, they flit from one focus to another without
spending enough time in any one area to learn anything very
well. Since paying attention is an important part of learning, by
definition, these youngsters have trouble learning. But we see

many hyperactive kids who, one way or another, learn to do their three R's pretty well. They are just inefficient learners who often don't know the answers because they didn't hear the questions.

Their distinguishing characteristics are often like those of the learning disabled child, only more severe.

They tend to be insecure and thus seek constant gratification. They are clinging vines.

They listen poorly, garble directions or requests, have very little tolerance for anything that seems difficult, and rarely stick to any task very long.

They show very bad timing. They are inappropriate in their activities because they are insensitive to their surroundings. Often this leads to being ridiculed, which reinforces a sense of persecution.

Typical of many troubled learners, Billy was always in the center of trouble. Often, however, he arrived on the scene after the trouble had begun but before the teacher or parent who came to resolve the squabble. Billy was blamed for many of these happenings because the real offenders had left the scene before they were caught.

Many of these kids think they are not liked or loved, which, unfortunately, is often true. They can be difficult in any social setting—at school, on the playground, or at home. Over the years I have had many parents admit that they truly hate their hyperactive child because of the anguish or headaches he imposes on their lives. The parents quickly add that they feel very guilty about the hate they feel.

Some of these youngsters are heedless. They walk into any-thing without an awareness of potential harm.

Added to all of this is the fact that they get angry and frustrated because they simply don't enjoy many successes in life.

The brighter they are, the more creative they are about getting into trouble.

One of my bright troubled learners was participating in a research study which demanded several hours of psychological investigation once a week. At the end of each study session, Adam was rewarded with candy. Although I argued against this reward, it was a routine of the laboratory. On the final day of Adam's study period he demanded the candy store, not just a piece of candy, or he refused to complete the study. His learning during that study was a step ahead of the research team's.

The rules for helping troubled learners are very simple, but following them can be very difficult, since they must be followed all the time.

Your child is your responsibility, and for the most part no one is going to raise your child for you. That's one of the problems that has emerged over the past ten or fifteen years. Parents have assumed, or hoped, or expected, that if they walked away and hired others to look after their children, their children would evolve into functioning adults. Kids do grow up, but they must be reared by someone who cares.

Find out what the job is and get to it.

This usually means becoming aware of your youngster's capabilities and her needs. The troubled learner underscores this necessity. How are you going to help if you don't know what's wrong or what needs to be done? Find out what needs to be done and how to do it and go to work. And bear in mind that common sense goes a long way with children.

Below are some steps that need to be taken with the troubled learner over and above those already talked about in the early chapters of this book. These kids also need to learn how to verbalize, how to run and jump, how to show discipline, and all the rest. They will most likely advance more slowly and need more help.

Step 1. Understand the child's problem and his specific needs. Troubled learners may have speech difficulties, they may be more awkward, or they may be slower adapting to a classroom situation. This makes them different and it creates special needs. They will withdraw from the group setting and they might get angry. Do not be frightened, anxious, or defensive. Be positive. Find out what's wrong and what's needed to fix it. Never assume that someone else is going to take over for you. These children need an informed advocate.

Start early. If the child needs speech therapy at age three, see to it then.

Assume control. Seek professional advice, make sure it makes sense, and monitor treatment and progress.

Identify resources. Often services available to children are unused because parents are unaware of them.

Keep informed. Today's parents may have no time, but you need to make time for this child now, not tomorrow.

Step 2. Insecurity and poor self-esteem are major problems for the troubled learner. They arise from repeated failure. Security will develop as the result of caring and the acquisition of skills. The child needs to know he is wanted, but he also needs to succeed. Love must be balanced with independence. Show love but don't smother the child. Sometimes parents shelter the child and make life seem threatening. While learning, children will fail. It's good for them—that's how they learn. But they must be encouraged and know that support is there. If you protect the child from failure, you'll limit learning and make him fearful. If he falls down, he'll get up, and he'll do it more quickly if he knows that you're there.

Step 3. Be patient. Youngsters who have trouble learning need time, support, and patience. Parents get tired, too. That's expected. Don't panic. Many parents think the child has to be perfect today. There's plenty of time to get the job done successfully. Plan better so you can use your time wisely. Use plenty of reinforcement. Each step along the way must be learned and "overlearned." Skills, facts, and new experiences must be strengthened until the child has made them automatic. Use everyday experiences to reinforce learning. Get the child to explain or show what he has learned.

Step 4. Emphasize the positive. Never be negative with your child. You are trying to help her. Criticism doesn't help, it destroys. Praise the step taken and move on to the next. Never worry about an unsuccessful attempt. Too many parents dwell on the child's failures, which creates anxiety in both parent and child.

Teachers, like parents, get anxious about these children. Worse, they may verbally abuse them for answering incorrectly. This is called negative reinforcement and it's the best way I know to insure that the child never answers again.

Be concerned with the child's understanding first—speed and accuracy will come with practice. Johnny had twenty simple arithmetic problems to complete. He finished ten, all correctly, and received a "grade" of 50 percent. I explained to his teacher that he knows how to do the work, but he needs more time. He's not failing, he's learning very well, but he works slowly. Even his pace will improve, given time and support.

Step 5. Keep learning relevant and appropriate for the child's age. If you destroy his self-image he'll quit trying to learn. I cringe every time I see a fifteen-year-old who has a reading problem working with one of those "pat-the-fat-cat" readers. What self-respecting teenager wants to be caught with a reading primer? Get teenage material reworked into a simpler form so the youngster can learn and maintain a little self-respect. Children do not want to be different.

Step 6. Make enrichment a daily event in the life of your child. The troubled learner, with impaired avenues for learning, must rely upon enriching experiences to fill in the blanks. Parents should assume that all experiences are reinforcement of daily learning. Be more conscious of your interaction, use time more wisely, and strengthen associations to enforce learning.

Keep in mind that we need to learn the alphabet to read and write, but not to talk and listen and think.

Step 7. Make special time for your child while keeping a balance to enjoy your own time or time with your other children. Learn to shift gears, to make time for others, but make others participants in the life-style that supports your troubled learner. Constant attention to a single job makes you inefficient and resentful. Take a break and identify helpers. Care of the special learner can be consuming and tiring.

One of the problems that faces many single parents today is the lack of a support system, such as family, that can provide relief from the everyday job of child care. Everyone needs time for herself.

Step 8. If the troubled learner is hyperactive, consistency in applying the above steps must be carefully applied. Hyperactive children need an extra hug, more reinforcement, and more patience. Look for support within or outside the family to make the plan work. If this means sharing "things that work" with other mothers of ADD children, find a group or create one. Make time to communicate often with your child's teachers to share experiences and develop strategies that meet his needs at school and at home.

Step 9. Timing is a critical skill for the troubled learner because of her tendency to overlook social signals. Be fair, be honest, and be appropriate. Explain and teach appropriate behavior. Get the child to think through a course of action to reinforce her understanding. Make her assume responsibility so that she assumes consequences; this allows decision making without paranoia. Get her to think before speaking or acting.

Step 10. Child development has four steps:

1. Do for him.
2. Help him do.
3. Watch him do.
4. Let him do.

These steps carry the youngster from infancy to independence. For the troubled learner the steps take more time, but you still need to take them. Don't encourage independence before he's prepared, but don't hang on too long, denying your youngster the opportunity to develop the independence necessary for a successful life.

I'm not saying that it's easy, but it will work if you do!

Epilogue: Strategies for Today's Child

*For the education of children only the best
is good enough.*
—Z. Kodály

We must develop better ways to deal with our children. By "we" I mean parents, schools, doctors, and a host of less easily identifiable people who shape the environment of our kids.

There is an extraordinary amount of money allocated each year by the government to education. Less than 0.5 percent of that $250 billion–plus budget goes to early childhood education. Last year I spoke to some people who were in charge of state programs for preschoolers in order to generate greater interest in early-childhood programs. At the time there were limited funds available at the federal level for these programs, and interest in such programs is certainly not overwhelming. Admittedly, some educators are frustrated because of limited financial support from the government and others because of limited planning for early-childhood programs within the states.

Twenty years ago I was appointed a U.S. Department of Education fellow to examine children's learning. The fellowship began with a week or so in and around Washington, D.C., to become more familiar with the workings of our government. One day we met with the man who was then head of the House Ways and Means Committee. He controlled the money, so he was certainly a good person to meet. As the only physician in our group, I was interested in how the committee approved solutions to problems that were purely medical in nature. When I asked our host how the members of the committee made reasonable judgments about the issues for which they were allocating funds he responded, "It's very easy. You listen to those who shout the loudest about their program." I guess that was as good a statement about the lobbying system in Washington as you get.

Children in this country have not yet found an effective advocate, one who can shout loudly enough for them.

Getting help from Washington is not an easy job. Some congressmen and senators regard their mission as including children and education, but other issues always seem to keep the children's agenda on the back burner. Maybe no one knows where to begin or what to do. There has been much talk and no action. Another way of looking at the Washington message is that the government isn't going to give the necessary help. It is expected to come from the parents and families. It's time we all realized that no one is going to assume our job.

Three issues confront the family today: more mothers work, so that child care by other than the mother (or father) is a necessity; more families have a single parent as the head of the household; and more families are poor.

A lot of books have been written about these three issues. They were not intended to advise the public. At best, most were written to alert professionals who might care about the issues. They are statements about public policy, but I've already told you that we don't have one. We have a Head Start program which, for the most part, has been alive and fairly healthy for at least twenty-five years. Yet fewer than 50 percent of the children who are eligible to participate in the program do so; there is a lack of program availability in areas where Head Start is needed.

Social scientists interested in education and the poor often dwell on the idea that we must spend more money to correct existing problems. At least for the time being, that isn't going to happen, but we cannot ignore the need. The poor often lack the skills to use available services and that must be overcome. Parents need to be educated along with their children. Money and services must be used more wisely.

Child-care needs are not limited, however, to the poor. Working mothers in the middle class must have affordable and effective child care. Their children have lost access to their "teacher" at home and their skills are declining along with their less fortunate peers. Day care must support the developmental needs of children. It cannot be custodial care. These youngsters also need a "head start" that prepares them for the formal years of education.

The support system that will create an effective environment for the preschool and early-school child must involve a physician who focuses on child development; a workplace that plans and builds child-care capabilities into its facilities; child development specialists who create programs that support the needs of children and put those strategies to work in child-care facilities; and insurance companies that show the wisdom to allow payment for child care as part of health-care insurance programs because they understand that social and intellectual development are linked strongly to physical health.

This system of care does not replace the parent; it involves the parent. Child care outside the home is always a substitute situation. It is not meant to assume child-rearing responsibilities. These are the parent's responsibilities and must remain so. The active participation of the parent is essential to the success of a child-care program.

I must repeat the advice presented in the first chapter of this book: do not let anyone *educate* your child for you. It is your job to nurture your child's capabilities. It is also your obligation to develop in that child the beliefs and perspective on life that will allow him or her to grow into the adult you have in mind.

What about the school-age child? Can programs similar to Head Start that provide intellectual, social, and physical care be developed to meet their needs? Can schools assume more of a role in the care of the child? They can, but it demands the interest and involvement of the parent.

Should you wait for the local or federal government to step in and dictate the programs for children? That's probably not advisable. Your children will have grown up before everyone agrees on what should be done.

During times of economic downturn people's interests become more self-serving. This is best seen in local governance, where money gets tight and appeals for new money fall on deaf ears. Teachers are going without their usual raises. Schools are being asked to make unheard-of cuts in areas like sports.

There's a bright side to this local penny-pinching, however, because for the first time in years we are realizing that we must all find a better way. We must become creative and solve our problems.

The reason that I dwell on all of this is because I believe strongly that our child-care strategies have to come from us, not someone else. We are responsible for our own children and there's no one in sight who is going to assume our job of raising our children.

The needs of your children can't wait. There is a time in the life of a child when the foundation must be laid. The time to build skills and offer support is now. Once you assume the responsibility for your own child's development the unfolding of the child's potential will happen for you.

The message is clear. The needs of our children are evident. The job to be done is ours to do. It can be accomplished if we accept it.

Trust yourself. Start now.

About the Author

James J. A. Cavanaugh, M.D., has devoted a professional lifetime to the care of children and has spent the past twenty-five years focusing on the ways in which parents can raise successful children. A graduate of Georgetown University Medical School, he completed his pediatric training at the Johns Hopkins Hospital in Baltimore and was a research fellow at Harvard Medical School and Massachusetts General Hospital in Boston. He has served as chief of pediatrics at St. Elizabeth's Hospital in Boston and has been a consultant to the Boston city schools. He has also been a senior postdoctoral fellow for the U.S. Office of Education at Harvard Medical School and at M.I.T., studying reading and language acquisition in children, and has done postdoctoral studies in developmental psychology at Brandeis University.

A pioneer in the development of programs in public and private schools for children with learning problems, Dr. Cavanaugh has lectured and written extensively. He created a child development program called BASICS for parents and professionals, and that program forms the foundation of this book. Dr. Cavanaugh now lives and practices medicine on Cape Cod.

171